"This book should be considered required reading for analysts, managers and executives seeking to drive business performance and gain competitive advantage through data-driven strategy and decision making. Dr. Haimowitz has distilled his considerable experience into a practical how-to guide that is sure to become a fundamental reference text for the modern analytics practitioner or manager, regardless of industry."

Zaheer Benjamin, *Group Leader in Business Intelligence & Analytics across Life Sciences, Broadcasting, and Major League Sports*

DATA ANALYTICS FOR BUSINESS

Interest in applying analytics, machine learning, and artificial intelligence to sales and marketing has grown dramatically, with no signs of slowing down. This book provides essential guidance to apply advanced analytics and data mining techniques to real-world business applications.

The foundation of this text is the author's 20-plus years of developing and delivering big data and artificial intelligence solutions across multiple industries: financial services, pharmaceuticals, consumer packaged goods, media, and retail. He provides guidelines and summarized cases for those studying or working in the fields of data science, data engineering, and business analytics. The book also offers a distinctive style: a series of essays, each of which summarizes a critical lesson or provides a step-by-step business process, with specific examples of successes and failures.

Sales and marketing executives, project managers, business and engineering professionals, and graduate students will find this clear and comprehensive book the ideal companion when navigating the complex world of big data analytics.

Ira J. Haimowitz, Ph.D., is Vice President of Product Management at Deloitte Consulting, specializing in developing and delivering strategy and analytics solutions for the life science industry.

Standard Legal Description

Deloitte refers to one or more of Deloitte Touche Tohmatsu Limited ("DTTL"), its global network of member firms, and their related entities (collectively, the "Deloitte organization"). DTTL (also referred to as "Deloitte Global") and each of its member firms and related entities are legally separate and independent entities, which cannot obligate or bind each other in respect of third parties. DTTL and each DTTL member firm and related entity is liable only for its own acts and omissions, and not those of each other. DTTL does not provide services to clients. Please see www.deloitte.com/about to learn more.

Deloitte Profile

Deloitte provides industry-leading audit and assurance, tax and legal, consulting, financial advisory, and risk advisory services to nearly 90% of the Fortune Global 500® and thousands of private companies. Our professionals deliver measurable and lasting results that help reinforce public trust in capital markets, enable clients to transform and thrive, and lead the way toward a stronger economy, a more equitable society, and a sustainable world. Building on its 175-plus year history, Deloitte spans more than 150 countries and territories. Learn how Deloitte's more than 345,000 people worldwide make an impact that matters at www.deloitte.com.

Disclaimers

This communication contains general information only, and none of Deloitte Touche Tohmatsu Limited ("DTTL"), its global network of member firms or their related entities (collectively, the "Deloitte organization") is, by means of this communication, rendering professional advice or services. Before making any decision or taking any action that may affect your finances or your business, you should consult a qualified professional adviser. No representations, warranties, or undertakings (express or implied) are given as to the accuracy or completeness of the information in this communication, and none of DTTL, its member firms, related entities, employees or agents shall be liable or responsible for any loss or damage whatsoever arising directly or indirectly in connection with any person relying on this communication. DTTL and each of its member firms, and their related entities, are legally separate and independent entities

DATA ANALYTICS FOR BUSINESS

Lessons for Sales, Marketing, and Strategy

Ira J. Haimowitz

Routledge
Taylor & Francis Group

NEW YORK AND LONDON

Designed cover image: gorodenkoff

First published 2023
by Routledge
605 Third Avenue, New York, NY 10158

and by Routledge
4 Park Square, Milton Park, Abingdon, Oxon, OX14 4RN

Routledge is an imprint of the Taylor & Francis Group, an informa business

© 2023 Taylor & Francis

The right of Ira J. Haimowitz to be identified as author of this
work has been asserted in accordance with sections 77 and 78 of the
Copyright, Designs and Patents Act 1988.

ISBN: 978-0-367-28150-2 (hbk)
ISBN: 978-0-367-28148-9 (pbk)
ISBN: 978-0-429-30036-3 (ebk)

DOI: 10.4324/9780429300363

Typeset in Bembo
by codeMantra

CONTENTS

About the Author   *ix*
Foreword   *xi*
Acknowledgments   *xv*

Part I Organizational Design Principles   **1**

1 Linking Business Challenges to Big Data Solutions   3

2 Selling the Big Data Analytics Initiative   14

3 Organizational Structures for Advanced Analytics   28

4 Lessons Learned Managing Big Data Departments   39

Part II Analytics Business Applications   **49**

5 Segmentation: Categorizing Your Customers   51

6 Targeting: Getting it "Right"   64

7 Campaign Measurement with Learning Objectives   75

8 Strategic Text Mining   91

9 Predictive Modeling for Business   102

Part III Implementation and Delivery 119

10 Privacy Considerations for Big Data Analytics 121

11 Delivering Results with Actionable Insights 128

12 Scalability and Long-Term Success 141

References *155*
Index *159*

ABOUT THE AUTHOR

Ira J. Haimowitz, PhD, is Vice President of Product Management at Deloitte Consulting, specializing in developing and delivering strategy and analytics solutions for the life science industry. He combines AI and machine learning education from MIT and Cambridge University, with over 20 years of product leadership and consulting expertise. Throughout his career, Ira has led product development and client delivery functions at several manufacturers, marketing agencies and analytics consulting firms. Ira lives in New York City with his wife Barbara, and is always proud of his three college-educated, independent children Nathan, Eva, and Deb.

FOREWORD

The Growth of Applied Data Science in Business

As the business world marches through the 2020s, one undeniable trend has been the proliferation of big data and data science programs at both universities and corporations. This, in turn, has been driven by hiring needs at employers with ever-growing data troves, feeling that analytics can drive company revenue, profitability, and growth (Davenport and Harris 2007; Hagiu and Wright 2020; Harris and Tayler 2019; Iansiti and Lakhani).

Accordingly, we have seen a rise in short courses, instructional books, and online certificate programs in *data science, predictive modeling, machine learning, and artificial intelligence.*

What is often missing for these newly trained professionals and analysts is guidance on how to apply these analytics techniques to real-world business applications. New analytics professionals lack the shared experiences and lessons learned of practitioners that have worked in applying big data across industries. Conveying these experiences is the objective of this book.

I've been fortunate to have worked over 25 years in multiple leadership capacities of applied analytics, across ten corporations, mostly in sales and marketing functions. These experiences have covered industries including healthcare, consumer packaged goods, financial services, retail, media, and communications. I've lived the perspective of both sides of the analytics projects:

- *Clients,* meaning manufacturers or advertisers of products
- *Service providers,* which include companies such as data suppliers, analytics consultants, advertising agencies, and public relations firms.

Additionally, I've worked across the broad scale of company sizes, from multinationals with hundreds of thousands of employees to co-located, growing entrepreneurial firms of under 50 employees. With this experience, I have compiled a knowledge base of analytics techniques, and project management skills for applying data science to sales, marketing, and strategy objectives.

Intended Audience for This Book

The topic of applying big data analytics to sales and marketing has been growing dramatically in the past 10 years. This book should have wide appeal in both the university and corporate settings. The book will be valuable as a text in bachelor's, master's, and certificate programs in Business Analytics that have been dramatically rising across universities in recent years.

The text should also prove valuable to corporations that provide analytics consulting or develop data-driven decision support products leveraging multi-dimensional data assets. There is ample guidance provided on how to best communicate with and deliver results to clients, whether those are one's own company's stakeholders or external customers.

The presumption is that the reader will have at least some minimal exposure to business, sales, and marketing objectives, as well as fundamental statistics. Some familiarity with data mining techniques is expected, but if not, the definitions of most analytics methods are spelled out as they are introduced. References to textbooks providing additional methodological depth are provided where required, or where the reader may wish a deeper understanding.

While the principles to be espoused here are driven by experience in sales and marketing applications (the focus of this book), many lessons and guidelines should also be applicable across business functions, including communications, research and development, operations, or finance. Across these departments are basic commonalities of applying quantitative analytics to challenging business problems.

Flow of This Book by Chapter

When I was a graduate student in computer science at MIT during the 1990s, many faculty and researchers recommended a classic book called *The Mythical Man-Month: Essays on Software Engineering*, by Frederick Brooks Jr (Brooks 1995). This was a collection of essays dating back to the 1960s from one of the early experts in the nascent field of large-scale software engineering, who had learned his trade in part during the mainframe heyday period of IBM. Each essay was self-contained and comprised lessons learned from a seasoned practitioner, intended as sound advice for newcomers to this technical field.

In the same spirit, I have written this collection of essays, hoping to receive a fraction of the acclaim that Mr. Brooks attained. Each chapter of this book is an educational essay that summarizes experiences and lessons learned in applying big data analytics to sales and marketing applications across industries. I've aimed for each essay to combine some formal definitions and frameworks, supplemented with realistic case studies, best practices, trade-offs, and guidelines.

This book consists of twelve chapters organized into three parts, aligned with business objectives. The first part covers lessons on organizational design principles. Included are chapters on translating business needs into analytics frameworks, selling a big data initiative to gain support and funding, organizational structures of commercial analytics groups, and management of big data departments. These chapters should be especially valuable to new leaders aspiring to launch and grow an advanced analytics department.

The second part probes Analytics Business Applications, consisting of five chapters on major disciplines driving sales, marketing, and strategy. These include segmentation, targeting, campaign measurement, text mining, and predictive modeling. For each of these chapters, there are formal definitions, realistic examples, evaluation methods, and insights on how sales and marketing organizations can best exploit these techniques.

The third part covers implementation and delivery, dealing with practical considerations for helping your advanced analytics function produce impactful results. The first two chapters in this section cover consumer privacy and its effect on implementation options, as well as trade-offs among the various methods of analytics delivery. The final chapter outlines the challenges and successes I've seen in achieving *scalable growth*. Indeed, as your company meets ever-increasing demand and success from its big data analytics capability, there are core focus areas that are essential to keep pace with that demand. These include automation, efficiency, quality control, and knowledge management.

The chapters each enumerate one or more anonymized case studies from sales and marketing to demonstrate the applicability of each topic. These scenarios do not indicate any particular companies, products, or individuals, and given the breadth of my experience, no specifics should be inferred from any use cases.

Each of the chapters is followed by a small set of exercises that can be assigned as homework in a formal class, or can be explored independently for the individual reader. There is a mix of quantitative questions with clear-cut answers, as well as assignments asking for linkage between one's own business experience and the principles and case studies within the chapter.

A Final Thought

The writing of a nearly 200 page textbook on technology applied to business must inevitably make choices on style or level of detail. Alas it is not possible to please all audiences, especially those seeking either depth of algorithms and coding detail or those seeking a breezy business best-seller. This book aims to strike a balance between those tones. The hope of this humble author is that by absorbing these selections, the reader will come away with applicable lessons to either launch or accelerate their practice.

ACKNOWLEDGMENTS

This book was a labor of several years and would not have been possible without the steadfast support of multiple organizations and close personal contacts.

The publishing team at Taylor and Francis and Routledge press has been most supportive and patient as I worked through the early stages of this manuscript, and later as my writing gained momentum and focus. I also appreciate their extensive help in editorial review, publishing, and marketing. That said, any errors that may exist within these pages are my responsibility alone.

Professional colleagues and friends that I admire have offered their encouragement and are too many to enumerate. At the beginning stages, former co-authors and colleagues Tim Keyes, Foster Provost, Patrick Moriarty, and Alan Bowman each served as initial reviewers of the book concept and outlines and provided valuable suggestions.

Several companies provided me support to work on this book while employed there, and also provided stimulating environments of diverse business problems requiring big data solutions. Note that any case studies referenced here are anonymized, and deal with general principles I have learned throughout my career, dating way back to my graduate studies at MIT and Cambridge; The range of academic and corporate experiences has shaped my perspectives that melded into this book.

My family has been steadfast in their love and support throughout this odyssey, especially my exceptionally talented wife Barbara, and my three scholarly children Nathan, Eva, and Deborah. They all provided emotional support, occasional editorial or research assistance, and periodic granting of solitude when I needed to focus. For these favors, I owe everlasting gratitude.

PART I
Organizational Design Principles

1

LINKING BUSINESS CHALLENGES TO BIG DATA SOLUTIONS

Upon graduation with my PhD, I made a determination to enter the corporate world, joining what was then one of the premiere applied research centers in the world at General Electric Corporate Research and Development. The primary reason for my choice was the potential to apply my freshly minted education in artificial intelligence and data mining to create inventions that solve real-world business challenges.

Over 25 years later, I have been neither disappointed nor bored with this decision. As I have worked across industries and spent time employed by manufacturers, agencies, data providers, and analytics consultants, there has been no shortage of fascinating business challenges to solve by developing innovative solutions leveraging large data sets.

1.1 Fundamental Differences between Academics and Business

There are significant differences between the academic environment where many new professionals are trained in data science and the business world where that training must be put into practice. We summarize these differences in Table 1.1 and will later go into more depth.

First, the data sets typically used in training are well studied, cleansed, and have all components merged together. Consider, for example, the Iris classification data set (Fisher 1936) containing several hundred observations from three types of flowers and four length measurements, used for teaching clustering, or unsupervised learning. All the variables required are summarized in one small table. By contrast, in the business world, data is dispersed usually among separate customer demographic, transaction, and product specification files, each with differing completion rates, time periods, and business rules for

DOI: 10.4324/9780429300363-2

TABLE 1.1 Primary Differences in Data Science Training vs Business Applied Analytics

Dimension	Data Science Training	Business Applied Analytics
Data complexity	Cleansed, integrated	Messy, disjointed, unstructured
Methodologies required	Specific analytic techniques	Hybrid approaches
Nature of requests	Framed by methods	Motivated by business goals
Constraints on solutions	Relatively few	Multiple

interpretation. Then separately is the rise of "unstructured" text data including social media and blog posts, or survey responses, which require dedicated pre-processing before business analysis can commence.

Second, the methodologies referred to in data science training tend to be isolated while taught. One section of classes may discuss classification models, another forecasting, and yet another natural language processing. Again, the data sets are prepared to match these specific objectives. In the business world, the methodologies needed for solving a particular problem will require more creativity and hybrid solutions. For example, early in my career as I applied analytics to financial services, an assignment came up that was fascinating and yet deceptive in the simplicity of the request:

• Assign credit terms to new small business accounts applying for retail credit cards.

This seemingly concise request, in fact, required a three-part hybrid solution:

1. Understand and segment the previous behaviors of businesses upon receiving credit.
2. Predict for a new credit applicant the probabilities of filling each behavior.
3. Optimize the credit terms for this new applicant to achieve maximal value for the company.

More details on an analytical solution to this challenge are provided in Haimowitz and Schwartz (1997); see also Provost and Fawcett (2013). We will provide deeper descriptions on this particular business application in Chapter 5 on segmentation applications. For now, let's return to Table 1.1 and address the final two points of difference between academic data science training and the complex business environment.

In academic training, the assignments are specific to the methods being learned. For example, if the coursework is related to the classification of unstructured text data into topics (such as sentiment levels), then the data set is specific to that challenge, it may be a corpus of Twitter social media posts related to a consumer brand, ready to be classified. Then, the data scientist could learn how to apply any of a series of methods to determine if each Twitter post was positive, negative, or neutral: keyword matching, statistical correlations, natural language parsing and semantics, supervised neural networks, or a combination of these. The learning is focused on the techniques and their tradeoffs, and therefore the data set and the assignment's objectives are kept clean.

By contrast, the business world might have a much broader request that is underspecified from a methodology standpoint. Staying within the same general theme as the above example, a popular consumer packaged goods client may approach a public relations company, and ask "what is our reputation among the public?" Then the PR firm could approach this problem of evaluating a brand's reputation in a variety of ways, including market research surveys, social media analysis, evaluation of relevant consumer blogs and forums, and product market share analyses. The prioritization of these various approaches will be based on available data, available staff, and project scoping.

Finally within the above table of differences in big data projects is the broad set of *solution constraints* that the corporate world imposes upon any significant analytics endeavor. In academic training, you have the latitude to develop the most accurate solution with little bounds on time or methodology. However, in business there are additional limitations that are placed upon the results of big data analytics projects. What drives these constraints?

1.2 Post-Analysis Business Process

To better enumerate and understand the constraints that applied big-data analysts face, consider how the results are utilized. What I've come to realize across my decades of experience is that analytics results are *not the end state* of a process, they are often the *beginning step of a business process enhancement*. The sequence of steps is illustrated in Figure 1.1.

As shown in the figure, after a quantitative study is completed by the analytics group (whether internal corporate or external vendor), the analytics leaders must shepherd the results through a series of follow-up stages.

1. First, the findings, insights, and implications must be presented to functional stakeholders in sales, marketing, and operations groups.
2. Second, the (perhaps updated) results need to be integrated within a company system for operational usage. This might mean a digital programmatic auctioning system, a salesforce automation system, or a business intelligence dashboard. Even something as simple as a reporting spreadsheet has to be planned for consistency with current business distribution.

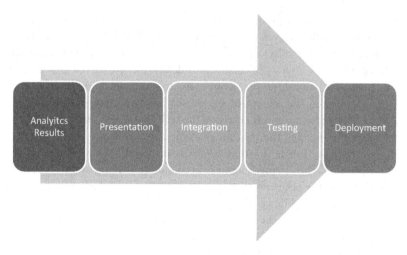

FIGURE 1.1 Business Process Drivers of Analytics Constraints

3. Third, these integrated results have to be tested for quality, operational efficiency, and acceptance. This might be on a pilot group of users, such as the sales representatives in a limited territory.
4. Finally, deployment across a broader scale of business users for maximal impact, such as the full regional (or national) sales force.

When I was in academia, often we would mark success of our innovative analytics models through the feasibility demonstration on several test cases. Further validation would come from peer-reviewed publications and presentations at academic conferences. As can be seen with the above sequence, the bar of successful deployment is quite different and more collaborative in the business world. For this reason, increasingly university Master's programs in Data Mining (Han and Kamber 2006) or Data Science are partnering with corporations for joint term projects as components of capstone courses.

1.3 Constraints upon Big Data Applications

Besides the multi-stage deployment process, we can enumerate the constraints that applied data science practitioners face even in performing the underlying analyses. These are illustrated in Figure 1.2, and we will describe and exemplify each within this section.

- *Time-based campaign milestones*: By far the most prevalent constraint on data mining projects is limitation of time. Applied analytics are intended to be deployed in the marketplace, and delays can result in loss of selling opportunities or missed competitive advantage. In addition, as described

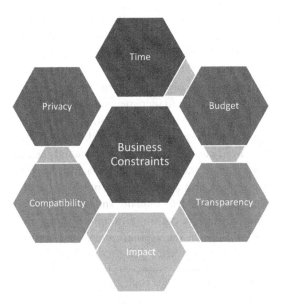

FIGURE 1.2   Business Constraints on Big Data Analytics Projects

in the previous section, several stages are required before the analytics results can be deployed. The corollary is that deadlines for analytics delivery often are derived through working backward from final deployment dates.

- On the corporate side, I've had to plan my schedule working backwards from major national sales meetings, needing to have analytics results reviewed by multiple layers of sales management well in advance, followed by having statistics incorporated into the field force materials.
- On the supplier side, a relevant example for timing is launching a media campaign, with deadlines usually dictated by client schedules. For example, if a major advertiser is launching new branded media campaign, then the analysis results have to be ready to devise the strategy and the creative execution, and the analytics system must be built to measure the campaign impact.
- *Limited budget*: Closely associated with time constraints are budget limitations. I've especially experienced this working for agencies and analytics consulting firms, where our costs were billed to clients based on hourly staffing rates. That is the true environment where "time equals money." Customers have a limited budget for analyses, which, in turn, drives the need for efficiencies of both lower hourly rates and shorter time to delivery. The reduced cost and shorter timing, in turn, place increased emphasis on selecting the right methodology and reducing high-risk, uncertain experimentation.

- *Demonstrable impact*: In the business world, innovative analytics will only be adopted if marketing and sales executives are convinced that making decisions based on the results will bring demonstrable business impact, such as increased revenue or reduced costs. Innovation for its own sake is not a luxury business can allow. This behooves a big data analytics project team to show how the outcomes of analysis can lead to incremental revenue, efficiency, or both.
- *Explainable methodology*: Very few organizations I've either worked for, or served as clients, can accept on faith a "black box" data mining solution. Rather, experienced customers want to understand the data sources, how information is collected and merged, what machine learning and modeling techniques are applied, and whether the results have statistical significance. Consequently, be prepared to explain and defend such details early on when selling in projects, all the way through final delivery.
- *Operational compatibility*: In the business world, big data project results are not achieving full impact when a presentation gets department head support and then sits on a shelf. Rather, results must be integrated into the sales or marketing business process. Through the years, I and my team have had to deploy artificial intelligence results within a host of systems, including banking mainframe computers, sales force automation systems, online campaign tracking dashboards, and digital trading desks. These implementations are not straightforward and require collaboration with operations leaders and training from associated vendors.
- *Consumer privacy*: This constraint indicates that personally identifiable information cannot be utilized in either the analysis or the delivery of the big data results. Often fields such as demographics, geography, income, and employment status are utilized as predictive variables or "overlays" to add additional insights within big data analytics. However, unless permission is granted by consumers, results need to be aggregated into generalized cohorts when showing results or taking marketing actions. We address consumer privacy issues specifically in Chapter 10.

1.4 Translating Between Two Perspectives

Having established these differences between big data analytics in academic training vs. the business world, let's delve deeper into a specific skillset required of corporate big data analytics professionals: translation of business requests into analytics specifications.

Executives leading sales or marketing functions require the support and partnership of analytics leaders to make informed decisions and stay competitive. Thus, collaboration is critical between these parties. However, due to different education, training, and experience, they communicate with different perspectives. The business executive speaks in terms of *goals and objectives*, whereas the analytics leader requires *detailed specifications* in order to contribute to those goals.

For example, the vice president of marketing with responsibility for a portfolio of multiple brands does not frame a problem during a meeting with a phrase like:

> Please fit a logistic regression model over consumer level demographics to predict future customer conversions.

The request is almost never that prescriptive. Rather the framing is usually in business terms such as:

> We need to acquire another one million members into our loyalty credit card program, with likely high spend and relatively low risk profiles. How can we accomplish this in three months?

These phrases or requests appear to come from two different languages, spoken in a dialogue between professionals of different backgrounds and priorities.

As such, a critical skill for any applied big data professional is to translate such open-ended business objectives to an *analytics specification* and project plan utilizing specific analytics techniques. This is illustrated in Figure 1.3. An incoming business request needs to be translated into a specification, or requirements list, that will help solve that problem, using these important factors:

- The *domain knowledge* of that particular industry, including terminology, reliable information sources, and decision-making criteria

Analytics Specification

FIGURE 1.3 Translating a Business Request into an Analytics Specification

- The *market context* of the competitive environment for the relevant brand and category, including where the relevant brands are within their lifecycle, market shares, product pipelines and upcoming launches, sales trends, etc.

An informative and groundbreaking article in *Harvard Business Review* based on a McKinsey study recognized this critical service provided by analytics groups, coining a role of *Analytics Translators* (Henke et al. 2018). The role is defined and articulated thusly:

> ...translators play a critical role in bridging the technical expertise of data engineers and data scientists with the operational expertise of marketing, supply chain, manufacturing, risk, and other frontline managers. In their role, translators help ensure that the deep insights generated through sophisticated analytics translate into impact at scale in an organization.

Thus, the analytics translators take the business-focused requests of sales and marketing leaders and convert them into project guidelines for the analytics team to commence work. In agency terminology, one might say this function creates a *brief* for the analysis.

Let's consider how your group can develop that translation capability, by providing examples and a guide that bridges between core business problems and analytics techniques.

1.5 Taxonomy of Sales and Marketing Objectives

Sales and marketing business leaders are responsible for a broad range of goals that can potentially be advanced through big data analytics. We can organize these objectives into categories, then for each category we can specify appropriate data sources and analytics methods which are applicable.

To provide a bit of context, let's flesh out a simple marketing example.

Consider a typical marketing environment where company C manages a portfolio of products P_1, P_2, ..., P_N across N different categories. For example, a large consumer packaged goods company may have products in these categories: carbonated beverages, bottled water, salty snacks, and breakfast food.

To illustrate one particular category, see Figure 1.4, where a brand has two main competitors in that category, and trails in market share to both of them. The figure shows market perceptions of important features A and B for all three products. As can be seen, one reason why Competitor 2 has top market share is because it leads in the two main product features. By contrast, the company's brand trails significantly in Feature A with a negative market perception, which helps make it the lowest market share product, despite a fairly high score in Feature B.

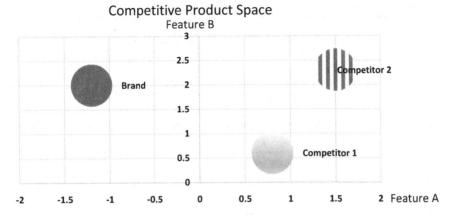

FIGURE 1.4 Basic Competitive Product Positioning with Market Shares

Given this context, let's divide sales and marketing business goals into two types, *marketplace intelligence* and *campaign design*. Below are some examples of how business requests can be mapped to advanced analytics approaches for each of these types.

- *Marketplace intelligence* includes gaining an understanding of the category, the customers and prospects, and the competitive environment. A brand leader would see the data in the figure above and recognize that they are trailing competition badly, and need to gain additional understanding. This need gives rise to the questions and associated analyses provided in Table 1.2.
- *Campaign design,* by contrast, deals with what in-market actions can a product marketing team take, presumably to grow the category size, or to gain share vs. competitors. Also important is the need to measure the effectiveness of those in-market actions and continually optimize for impact and cost efficiency. These needs give rise to an alternate set of questions and analytics frameworks provided in Table 1.3.

TABLE 1.2 Analytics Translation for Marketplace Intelligence

Business Question	Analytic Framework
How large is the potential market?	Market sizing, forecasting
Where are we winning and trailing?	Market share analysis, customer behavioral segmentation, factor analysis, principal components, clustering
How can we reach our prospects?	Promotional channel research, indexing
What are our competitors saying to stakeholders?	Competitive intelligence transaction analysis, text mining
What is the customer journey of our prospects?	Path and network analyses, source of business, state transition modeling

TABLE 1.3 Analytics Translation for Campaign Design

Business Question	Analytic Framework
Who are the most important prospects to reach?	Customer segmentation and targeting, path analysis
How can I best reach these priority customers?	Propensity modeling, channel selection, next best action; message content analysis
How do I know whether my promotion is working?	Campaign measurement, ongoing monitoring, and promotional optimization

In the chapters ahead, this textbook will provide more depth on nearly all of the analytics techniques mentioned above. There will be descriptions of the problem framing, required data preparation, methodology, and interpretations. Those details will provide the follow-up actions for an analytics translator to convey to their advanced analytics group.

One final note: simple lookup tables for business analytics translation are only the first step to solving complex business objectives with big data analytics. What must follow are detailed requirements gathering, both via personal interviews, workshops, scenario planning, and automated data extraction. Those requirements, in turn, help shape the critical parameters for executing the advanced analytics methods, as well as the success criteria for judging results. These too are the topics of subsequent chapters.

1.6 Conclusion

This chapter introduces some of the major dichotomies in training and staffing big data analytics organizations. First is the difference between academia and the business world. Then, within the commercial business world, we examined distinctions between "clients," or manufacturers and advertisers, and suppliers like agencies, data suppliers, and analytics consultants. Then drilling down further and considering specific big data projects, we recognized that there is a different language for business objectives than there is for analytics project planning and methodology. The skills of the analytics translator are to employ creativity and efficiency to navigate between these two languages adeptly and effectively bring business impact from deep quantitative analyses.

1.7 Exercises

1. Consider a big data analytics project you are currently involved in, or planning for the near future. As described in Figure 1.1, what are the stages of post-analysis delivery that you anticipate? Who are the collaborators and stakeholders you have to work with at each stage? How does each of these stages impact and constrain your analytics results?

2. Describe a request you have received from an internal (or client) business executive where you had to serve as an analytics translator. Show step by step how you converted the business-oriented request into a project specification and plan.

3. Consider the simple competitive landscape described among the three products in Figure 1.4. Presume that you are the director of the marketing team for the brand.

   a) Name two priority questions you would want answered by the next quarterly review.

   b) Using the tables in Section 1.4 for analytics translation, what types of projects might you ask your big data analytics suppliers to provide?

2
SELLING THE BIG DATA ANALYTICS INITIATIVE

This chapter will help business executives justify to their management the investment in large-scale analytics initiatives. Some of the factors we will cover are:

- Creating a long-term vision and a multi-year plan to attain it
- Alignment with the company's strategic objectives and critical needs
- Choosing pilot projects that are impactful and achievable

2.1 Background: Why Justification Is Needed

With the tremendous growth of data capture by businesses, there has been associated pressure to produce new enterprise, corporate capabilities that utilize this data. In fact, I've seen this general business mandate for decades, What has changed is the evolution of the preferred architecture for large data stores: a shift has occurred from in-house data warehouses of mostly table-structured data to cloud-based repositories hosted by firms like Microsoft, Google, or Amazon, and a mix of structured and unstructured, including text, image, and video.

What has stayed the same is the need to *justify the business impact* of Big Data investments. Too many companies, now as then, tend to overpromise this potential impact, claiming extraordinary game changing successes in 1–2 years, or without any time horizon at all. A recent example from the business and technology headlines is the promise of IBM's Watson artificial intelligence system. A recent *New York Times* article summarizes this case study (Lohr 2021). During the 2010s, IBM advertising and public relations claimed that Watson would analyze high volumes of transactions to transform healthcare. Years

DOI: 10.4324/9780429300363-3

later, expensive contracts with major hospital systems bore little impact on patient outcomes.

Such exorbitant claims of big data analytics impact often lead to unreasonable expectations. How can this be avoided, so that business impact tracks along with big data investment?

2.2 A Working Example: B-to-B Software Development

Over my career, I've been on leadership teams for multiple companies that have tried to grow a data mining, or big data analytics capability. The working example below is fictitious yet realistic based on my experiences, and I hope it resonates with readers across sales and marketing functions. This scenario is anonymized but realistic, and we can call it "Intelligent Customer Engagement" (ICE).

Consider a fictitious mid-sized company called *Softech* which sells business-to-business workflow, cloud-based **CRM** and analytics software aimed at a broad user base across industries. Softech has expanded its data collection significantly of customer and prospect interactions across many touchpoints.

They are collecting, in disparate data feeds, the following information:

- Call center questions from customers and prospects
- Email correspondence from customers and Softech replies, both time-stamped
- Softech website logged in visits, linked to customer or prospect identifiers
- Chat bot interactions and responses
- Billing transactions, invoices, sales, and payment timeliness
- Customer contact information, including officers of each client company

Softech is supplementing this contact information with additional third-party data sources on these corporations from credit agencies and external sales leads. This information includes parameters like:

- Years in Business
- Annual sales
- Executive contacts
- Business lines and industries
- Number of employees
- Credit rating

Proponents of the Softech Intelligence Customer Engagement initiative know that further investment is required to integrate these disparate information sources, to achieve maximal benefit for Softech and its customers. More time, staff, hardware, and software investments will be required. To convince Softech management to fund such investment, they wish to link the project to several of Softech's corporate strategic objectives, covering revenue growth, risk management, and customer success:

1. *Customer Satisfaction*: Lead the industry of business enterprise software in customer satisfaction.
2. *Organic Top Line Growth*: Double annual sales per account, by increasing customer renewals combined with upselling services and enhancements beyond the primary product.
3. *Risk Reduction*: Dramatically reduce financial exposure by tightening credit policies and shortening customer time to pay.

Importantly, Softech has to determine how its expansion into big data analytics will support the achievement of its three-pronged corporate vision.

2.3 Linking Big Data Analytics to the Company Vision

Let's examine the components of the vision more closely to see what data are required, and what metrics must be defined, to achieve these goals and measure progress along the way.

Customer satisfaction is core to Softech's goals, admirably. From a big data perspective, two questions arise: how can analytics help improve customer satisfaction, and how can Softech measure that improvement? Let's cover those two in order.

Increased satisfaction can be achieved in many ways, but three methods of improving customer satisfaction through data are:

- *Relevant offers*: Say Softech has demographic data that a new client is a start-up firm in the office equipment business. Softech can offer this client a special "growing business package" for several users, including specialized training and supplementary tech support.
- *Personalized, continual communications*: Given a history of all its customer interactions at their fingertips, Softech can communicate in a tailored way based on previous questions, usage patterns, and professional roles of client contacts.
- *Improved quality:* As Softech delivers analytic dashboards across its customer base, it's critical to implement quality control, ensuring that results are correct and consistent. Errors are inherent in any human-built process, but must be documented, monitored, and reduced over time, as in a six-sigma program (Gitlow 2015; Oakland 2008). Decreases in errors generally bring increased customer satisfaction. The same can be said for reducing time delays.

Ultimately, to determine if customer satisfaction is improving, this has to be quantified and assessed routinely. Metrics can come from customer surveys, renewal rates, or the fashionable net promoter score (one to ten, likelihood to recommend). This data too should be collected for continual improvement.

Back to Softech, their next objective is achieving organic top-line growth, which means gaining renewals and expanded purchases from current customers. Here are ways the firm can leverage its big data assets to achieve this:

- Analyze transactional data from loyal, high volume customers, to understand patterns of what repeat and renewal customers order. Then assign new customers to the most likely pattern with classification models. Finally, leverage these results to recommend to new customers the most profitable and likely additional products. Figure 2.1 summarizes this approach and mentions specific analytic techniques that Softech can leverage with their historical customer data.

Finally, risk reduction is another core strategy for Softech. Exposure can be reduced by tightening credit terms, such as reducing available credit lines and reducing time to payment. However, how does Softech make sure that these policies are implemented for the right customers? After all, if credit is tightened across the board, this can severely hamper the other objective of top-line organic growth, especially in a competitive environment where other software firms have less stringent credit policies.

The answer comes back to using the customer demographic attributes and the transactional data. Softech can first develop profiles of those customers who have been credit risks, exhibiting late payment. Then, Softech can develop predictive models that estimate the likelihood, or the magnitude of risk for customers with those profiles. The customer data seems to already include a credit score from a third party. This can be used directly, or that score can be embedded in a more customized model for Softech specifically.

This methodology, not too different in principle from the marketing steps in the Figure 2.1, was in fact that I've developed in corporate retail financial services (for more details and a case study, see Haimowitz and Schwarz 1997).

Summarizing this section, it's apparent that the data investments underway by Softech can be instrumental in achieving corporate goals. Thus, there is the potential for alignment. Now, how do the leaders of the ICE initiative sell this within their company?

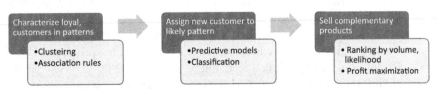

FIGURE 2.1   General Method for Organic Growth Leveraging Transactional History

2.4 Methods of Selling and Justification

Once you have spelled out how the additional data assets and associated analytics will contribute to key corporate objectives, you will have to convince executives with budget control of the value of further investment in this initiative. In my experience, part of your argument will be a major presentation that is in effect a business plan. Those who have led entrepreneurial environments will recognize many of the components listed below as core components of a pitch to seek investment. The sections below call out specific elements that I have found especially valuable in gaining endorsement for sales and marketing-related big data initiatives.

2.4.1 Personas and Storyboard Scenarios

Any large-scale data mining effort will effect your company's (or client's) way of working, and the experience of your customers. Thus in your selling argument, articulate who those people are that will benefit. One way to achieve this is through personas. Actually describe typical employees and customers whose lives will change once you have implemented your analytics-driven intelligence.

In multiple roles across companies, I've designed data-driven solutions for pharmaceutical sales organizations, including targeting, customer dashboards, sales rep digital sales aids, and digital relationship marketing programs. To explain the impact these solutions would have, I illustrated through fictitious but realistic personas, such as:

- Dr. Marilee Johnson, a cardiologist belonging to a leading specialty practice and also affiliated with the nearby university hospital.
- Kayla Walters, a sales representative with XYZ Pharma, who shows digital sales aids with the latest information to her physician customers, including Dr. Johnson.

With the personas defined, develop a storyboard, or sequence of events, describing how the personas would utilize a data-driven solution for efficiencies and a better experience. In the above example, analytics can enable these enhancements:

- Sales rep Kayla Walters might have additional information regarding Dr Johnson's education and affiliations.
- Ms. Walters might know the formulary status of different medications from XYZ Pharma at the hospital where Dr. Johnson has privileges.
- Dr. Johnson may have access to an online portal where she can view product information, see recent clinical trial results, and request samples for the practice.

- Those requests could in turn generate alerts to Ms. Walters, who could deliver the samples on her next call.
- Together, this storyboard brings to life in the executives' minds just how the major initiative will enhance business processes and either drive additional revenue or bring cost efficiencies.

2.4.2. Competitive Positioning Arguments

One very persuasive argument to get endorsement for a big data expansion is to claim improved product positioning relative to competition. For example, say you have evidence from customer surveys or industry benchmarks that your firm lags in customer service relative to other firms in your market. You may claim that collecting and utilizing enhanced customer data can help you provide better, more personalized service, and close the competitive gap on that critical feature.

Alternatively, consider if you can leapfrog the competition with your big data innovation. Say your chief competitor has a reputation among clients as delivering with a "set it and forget it" mentality, one size fits all delivery and then minimal attention to customer needs after first delivery Then your personalized service driven by enhanced data and predictive models can actually become a competitive advantage.

2.4.3 Project Roadmaps and Milestones

Part of selling a big data initiative is providing a project plan, or roadmap, showing expected progress over time. In any innovation I've brought to market, my executive leadership, or top clients inevitably ask, "when will this be ready?" This can be difficult to answer early in planning stages.

To provide transparency for the project and simplify answering the "when" question, break down the project into shorter yet significant components, whose completion times are milestones that are easier to estimate. The time granularity need not be too specific at the selling stage. Usually monthly, or even quarterly estimates can provide enough precision. Examples of these relevant called-out project stages can include:

- Stakeholder interviews and findings
- Initial database architecture design
- Software interface specifications
- First prototype complete
- Launch of new product or service
- Initial client delivery

Added to these may be additional key *company milestones* that are beyond your control but are critical to successful implementation and progression of your initiative. Examples of these are as follows:

- Annual brand planning for marketing groups, where you want to contribute new brand and marketplace insights leveraging your advanced analytics
- National and regional sales meeting where you may need to supply the field force with innovative customer intelligence, or training on your new data-driven account reports

Noteworthy as significant milestones are the design, implementation, and completion of pilot projects, executed within specific geographies or product lines. We give these pilots a detailed treatment in Section 2.5.

2.4.4 Revenue and Expense Forecasting

Since a big data analytics initiative is a financial investment, the ultimate decision-makers will want to see proof of a return on this investment. On numerous occasions, I have had to quantitatively justify early-phase investment with forecasts of future revenue increases or cost savings.

See Table 2.1 for a simplified example of such a financial model that you can include in your pitch for investment in your big data initiatives. The timescale in this table covers four periods, which typically represent fiscal years, but in an aggressive plan they can be quarters or half-years. The sections include Investments at top, which are costs, followed by Benefits beneath, with Benefits minus Investments defined as a Net Benefit.

Individual companies will vary in complexity demanded of such a financial model; we have kept this fairly general. Investments include costs for data,

TABLE 2.1 Elements of Basic Investment and Break-Even Model

Components	Estimates ($000s)			
	Period 1	Period 2	Period 3	Period 4
Investments				
Data, servers, and software	950	650	400	300
Staffing	300	400	450	550
Benefits				
Increased revenue	0	500	1,000	1950
Decreased marketing and customer service costs	0	100	200	350
Net benefit	(1.250)	(450)	350	1,450
Cumulative benefit	(1,250)	(1,700)	(1,350)	100

servers, and software, which are front loaded in Period 1 and then taper off to a lower, non-zero spend level. Also included is staffing level, which grows gradually over time. The Benefits section includes a line item for incremental revenue attributed to using the enhanced information. Also included are cost efficiencies, or savings for marketing and customer service, that might be met from increased automation.

In this model, Period 1 is marked by all Investment with no benefits, as is typical with a new venture, Then as time proceeds, investment drops slowly and benefits begin to increase, with increased revenue and also cost efficiencies kicking in. The bottom line of the model shows a Cumulative Benefit, where the summed Net Benefits over time show the total effect of the initiative. The break-even period is when the Cumulative benefit crosses from negative to zero, which occurs between Periods 3 and 4 in this simple case. To earn endorsement and funding for your big data initiative, the break-even period should be as soon as possible.

Finally, note a more sophisticated financial accounting would allow for a net present value of investment with interest rates, but that is omitted here – the goal is to teach the main concepts of a sales justification.

2.4.5 Cautionary Tales

As you prepare your presentation seeking endorsement for your big data initiative, there are challenging traps to avoid. I have seen technical leaders, including this author, stumble at times when raiming to quickly seek favor of their companies or clients

- *Avoid overpromising on timing*: The milestone calendar and schedule have to accurately represent your best knowledge of what innovations, deliverables, and impacts can be achieved each time period. Sometimes under pressure from one's management or clients, one can promise results too soon. Resist the urge to invent timings one cannot commit to. If the key decision-makers are insistent and you are uncertain, then pledge to study further and follow-up.
- *Express trade-offs when demands rise*: One of my favorite project management phrases is, "You can't have it good, fast, and cheap." This relationship is represented in Figure 2.2. If one aims to deliver to a milestone more quickly, either it will cost more money for the same quality, or maintain cost but reduce quality.
- It's the job of the overall program manager and visionary to know how to articulate such trade-offs. In your proposal, be ready to answer questions on how the advanced analytics can be cut, and how the storyboard will change, in the case of a timing acceleration at fixed cost, or under a reduced budget.

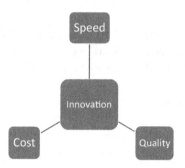

FIGURE 2.2 Fundamental Innovation Trade-Offs

- *Don't misrepresent your platform's capabilities*: The popular press and industry keynote speakers can hook audiences on future visions that can be confused for short-term realities. Also, other companies like your competitors can overstate their product features. You need not claim that your big data capabilities will automatically learn and improve its modeling over time, if that is not possible or intended. Better to state in clear business terms with technical transparency what can be achieved at each phase and milestone, because your group will likely get held to deliver on your claims.

2.5 Pilot Projects That Deliver Quickly

In my experience, it is rare that the full budget for a big data enterprise is approved immediately. Rather, success must be demonstrated early on a small scale in order to gain additional funding and support for scaling up. This demonstration can come in the form of *pilot projects,* small-scale combinations of analysis and implementation that can show a measurable benefit rapidly and yield lessons learned for future phases of scale-up (Thomke 2020).

Let's formalize what we mean: a big data pilot project is a short-term deployment of innovative data sources or analytically derived insights to solve a particular business problem among a small, self-contained group within a company. The pilot thus consists of the following components:

1. A working project team of colleagues or clients
2. Specific business objectives
3. A defined time window
4. Novel data sources or algorithms
5. An output, such as a report or dashboard
6. Derived actionable insights or recommendations
7. Metrics for evaluation of project success

In proposing the pilot project to stakeholders at your company, all of these components need to be clearly described and agreed to by the broader sponsors and project team.

2.5.1 Choosing a Pilot Project

How does one choose the small-scale environment for a pilot project? That will depend on your organizational design and support. For sales-driven organizations, an ideal place to start is picking a particular geography, overseen by specific district managers (for domestic) or country managers (for global projects).

Another option for pilot projects is to try a particular small-scale product for testing. I've piloted new data-driven methods for setting credit terms within a large financial services company, starting with a particular retailer's new private-label credit customers, and for a limited time period. Here too, relationships mattered, and it was essential to build trust with the retailers and credit managers, in part through transparency of what data and methodology were used, and keeping communication lines open.

2.5.2 Building a Cross-Functional Pilot Team

Having brought analytics innovations to large corporations as both an internal team leader as well as a consultant, I will strongly emphasize the importance of creating a cross-functional team before launching a pilot. Taking the time for gaining alignment and commitment early on will save potential delays later in your rollout.

Let's return to the example of a pilot field force intelligence initiative, and the importance of winning the support of specific district and regional sales managers. I've found these sales executives to be critical partners in driving the utilization of innovative customer dashboards or new targeting reports among their teams. Choose a sales team that is open to innovation, not afraid of missing quota, and prepared to give honest feedback after testing your data-driven results in their account management and messaging. From your end, offer to provide training, answer questions, and listen on customer calls to really find out how your new information is used.

To add some depth to this scenario we might choose our pilot project team to include a particular sales district within the U.S. Sales Division. Since this example is realistic but anonymized, let's call this the Charlotte North Carolina District. Fred, the District Manager is your critical partner for training and rollout of this pilot. Fred's 8 direct reports, the sales representatives, will be using this information for their selling in each of their territories. Other members of the team include the following:

- Colleagues from the Sales Operations group who will help you deploy the new advanced customer intelligence within the CRM sales platform. They are also critical partners in defining the project timelines.

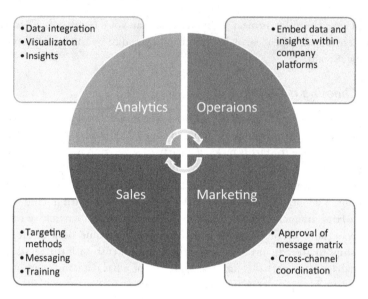

FIGURE 2.3 Members of the Cross-Functional Pilot Team

- The Marketing department, which will have specific recommendations on how particular analytics results are mapped to messages the sales reps should provide. For example, the direction could include how to message based on a client's upward sales trend for a newly launched competitor.
- Finally, of course the Analytics group at the corporation must be consulted. You want to make sure your big data results are consistent with prior analyses. Additionally, this team will be a critical partner in performing the analyses in future rollouts.

In summary, as shown in Figure 2.3, the pilot team will consist (at minimum) of members of these four key functions: Analytics, Operations, Sales, and Marketing.

Considering all of these roles is critical; each group must be informed of timelines, milestones, and progress. My suggestion is to appoint stakeholders from each of these groups on a steering committee and empower each committee member to offer critical feedback and communicate to their departments regarding pilot status.

2.5.3 Evaluating Outcomes of a Pilot

Evaluating the outcomes of the pilot project is critical to gaining further support for the entire Big Data initiative. A successful result on this initial phase will suggest further widespread rollout, and start planning for operational scale-up. Thus, the metrics have to be carefully planned in advance. Consider the following means of evaluation:

- *Pilot group feedback on information provided*: Since your objective is to leverage advanced analytics for organizational change, you've got to listen to the pilot group to find whether they have in fact changed. Do they understand your new information? Have they been following your recommended new customer service process? Be thorough and employ all the tools of market research: surveys, one on one interviews, and focus groups.
- *Usage and activity tracking*: As valuable as feedback sessions and surveys are, it's also important to actually collect activity tracking information to determine if the pilot groups is actually using your information. In the case of new reports, dashboards, or sales force automation systems, the metrics can come from downloads, clicks, and SFA navigation. With this information, you can actually correlate usage of your innovative metrics with improved performance (see below).
- *Performance metrics compared to a control group*: As mentioned on our section on sales justification, the key decision-makers expect either increased revenue, cost efficiency gains, or both. The pilot project is a chance to demonstrate this impact on a small scale.

Measure quantitatively these financial metrics, or proxies, for the pilot group using your new data-driven reports, dashboards, or platform, and compare them to a "matched control group" of a very similar make-up. One way to find such a control group is with a hold-out sample. In a financial services scenario, do not offer the promotional credit rate to every random fifth prospect that you would have, and see how that group behaves vs. the promoted group. Measure spending, purchases, and payment patterns for promoted and hold-out groups, and see how they change over time.

Another technique I've applied with sales force initiatives is "matched markets." In the US, match the pilot Dallas district to the control Houston district; or pilot in Cleveland and compare to Cincinnati.

In this way, follow the framework in Figure 2.4, and measure how the core impact metrics change from before the pilot duration to the end phases, once training and implementation are running smoothly. Incorporate a forecast of expected behavior for each group as well. If revenue, cost savings, or both are improved for the pilot group more than forecasted, ahead of the forecasted pace for the control, you have achieved a benefit.

If the small-scale pilot impact is demonstrated, and you are confident this can be scaled-up to your whole company's operations, then in your milestone presentation you may wish to extrapolate, projecting the impact companywide, or nationwide.

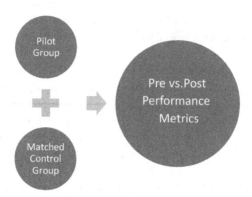

FIGURE 2.4 Evaluating Pilot Projects vs. a Matched Control Group

2.6 Conclusions

Selling a Big Data initiative to a client, or within your own company, is a major undertaking. One has to demonstrate a combination of relevance to the company mission, feasibility of execution, and financial impact. The presentation is akin to a full business plan including competitive analysis, project roadmap, financial forecast and scenario planning.

The payoff from all of this rigor is that you will have articulated the advanced analytics initiative so that executives in your firm can understand and relate to it. With proper selling, big data analytics will not be a technological curiosity, but rather a vital component of the corporate strategy. This accomplishment will make your sales effort worthwhile.

2.7 Exercises

1. Consider a strategic objective of your current company, one you've worked for previously, or one you're following in the news. Based on the lessons of this chapter:
   a)   How can the company align future big data initiatives to achieve its goals?
   b)   Flesh out a specific selling tactic that could convince the company's senior management to move forward with the big data effort.

2. Select a big-data initiative you have proposed or designed for your company, or a client. How can you describe the potential impact of this effort using personas and story boards:
   a)   Who are the key stakeholders that will benefit, and how would you describe them?
   b)   What are the ways that their jobs will be become easier, more efficient, or more profitable?

3. Consider the basic investment model of Table 2.1 that aims to justify investment in the Big Data initiative. Suppose the executives who hold the budget insist upon a faster time to break even, no later than three time periods. What changes could the business planner make to meet that more aggressive timeline? Describe this with realistic operational scenarios.

3

ORGANIZATIONAL STRUCTURES FOR ADVANCED ANALYTICS

3.1 Challenges to Growing a Department

As a result of your successful sales pitch (previous chapter), you have been provided funding to grow headcount in advanced analytics. Before you can start hiring though, there are several key questions that you must address:

- What are the business functions needed for this analytics department, and how should they be organized?
- Which data sources do you acquire and which can you delegate out to service providers?
- Do you hire internally, or pay consultants, agencies, or other service providers?
- Should you develop product development partnerships with other companies having complementary skills and assets?
- Where should various functional teams be located, relative to your corporate marketing headquarters?

These are questions without unique answers; indeed, the decisions you make can depend upon corporate culture, preferred working styles, and available time to reach critical mass. There are trade-offs related to speed vs. budget, and considerations related to intellectual property.

In this chapter, I will share lessons learned having worked for over 25 years growing and leading analytics functions across eight corporate environments, multiple industry sectors, and both within manufacturer (client) and supplier companies. I've worked for firms with over 100,000 employees within multiple analytics groups across departments; as well as companies with fewer than

DOI: 10.4324/9780429300363-4

100 people that were building data capabilities from scratch, one person at a time.

Across those positions, I've seen common capabilities replicated, that are required by advanced analytics groups. I have also seen some roles that are luxuries for larger departments, and not attainable by smaller groups just starting up.

3.2 Roles as the Building Block

One valuable lesson I learned early in my career as my department was expanding its analytics staff: do not think of headcount, think of *roles*. A role is a description of a set of responsibilities performed by the same individual. The person in this role can be anywhere from entry level to senior management, and the responsibilities can range from behind the scenes data science and analysis to client-facing account management.

Is each staff member assigned to exactly one role? Does a role have to be specific enough to an individual? That depends on the size of your company. Large corporations seeking to grow a function may create a role that multiple employees will fill. A mid-sized firm may assign a unique individual to each role. In small startups and growing firms under 100 people, as well as nimble agencies, certain critical staff members can fill multiple roles, until further revenue growth justifies clearer job differentiation. I have certainly been in these smaller types of environments, simultaneously selling capabilities, building products, and delivering to customers. Such a "multi-hat" work environment can alternate between exhilarating and exhausting.

Ultimately, a role in a big data, or advanced analytics, group consists of three main components, as indicated in Figure 3.1

- Place in the organization
- Responsibilities
- Skills

FIGURE 3.1 Components of a Role in a Big Data Organization

These have some dependencies, but are helpful to consider separately.

First, consider where this role fits within your company. Is this an individual contributor who will be hands-on? Is it a middle-level manager who will manage staff and oversee priorities across multiple projects? Or is this a senior-level executive who will help set vision and engage in long-term planning?

Also critical in specifying a role is articulating the core responsibilities of a person filling that role. Some critical responsibilities in a big data organization include:

- Development of analytical product components or functionality
- Operational responsibilities for delivery throughput or increasing scale
- Performing ad-hoc, or custom analysis
- Product ownership, managing the roadmap of features and functions over time.
- Translating client business needs into analytics specifications
- Delivery of analyses to clients
- Organizational
  - Supervisory responsibilities
  - Connections to other departments
  - Participation in major company initiatives

Each of the above responsibilities will have an expected skill set to execute successfully. These skills may include knowledge of programming languages, statistical techniques, project management frameworks, or business development experience. In the next section, we will articulate specific responsibilities as we describe key roles of an advanced analytics group.

3.3 Leading Roles in a Big Data Organization

Having built data-driven analytics and product groups across organizations large and small, I have identified a core set of roles that any manager should consider in building their teams. Per the previous section, let's describe each of them in terms of organization, responsibilities, and skills. Figure 3.2 shows an organizing principle of the roles, aligned on an axis from focus on data and analytics to a focus on business and clients. Our descriptions will proceed from "left to right" in this continuum.

3.3.1 Development Operations

Dev Ops staff are in charge of core infrastructure technology to support analytics and product development and in charge of maintaining data processing and storage for an organization. The storage may consist of a centralized data

FIGURE 3.2 Big Data Roles Organized by Focus Area

lake or warehouse. Alternatively, this may consist of a distributed, cloud-based storage architecture. The operations staff must balance various organizational objectives, such as cost efficiency of cloud computing vs. speed of access for analysts and data scientists. This group usually defines the data architecture, including the business-specific schemas within databases, and creation of data marts for specific analytics groups or decision support applications.

Some specific skills of data and development operations can include vendor management, extract, transformation and load (ETL) pipeline routines, and tactical efficiency measures like creating indexes on data tables for rapid access. Other critical areas of responsibility can include backup and archiving, information security, and disaster recovery.

3.3.2 Data Engineers

The data engineers are tasked with intimately understanding your company's raw input data sources, and with transforming that input data into usable components for business analysis. They need to be familiar with the sources of information, and assess how that source compares to competitive offerings. Data engineers share a responsibility with data operations to perform data quality analyses, judging if information is complete, accurate, and stable.

Some specific skills of data engineers may include:

- Building application programmer interface (API) hooks to external data sources for extracting and downloading files
- Creating natural language parsers, to extract features (like sentiment, or health keywords) from unstructured text data (such as social media or news feeds)
- Creating algorithms for imputation of missing data (filling in the blanks)

3.3.3 Data Scientists

The role of data scientists is to utilize the loaded and cleansed data to perform different types of analyses specific to the business objectives or the product specifications. Skill sets cover a spectrum, and range from what might be called *feature extraction*, at one end, *modeling* in the middle, and *insights generation* at the other end. With that continuum in mind, analysts should be adept at much of the list below:
Feature extraction techniques:

- Merging of separate tables (for which SQL is essential).
- Transformation and aggregation of variables.
- Statistical distribution calculations, often using specialized software packages such as in Python, R or SAS.
- Reporting on subtotals, frequencies, or cross-tabulations of key features.
- Sentiment labeling from unstructured text (such as positive, negative, or neutral).

Modeling techniques:

- Segmentation of observations into meaningful groups.
- Clustering, a type of unsupervised learning that creates distinct segments.
- Classification, assignment of observations into two or more segments.
- Predictive modeling, which creates functions that map multiple inputs into an output for decision-making.
- Python and R both have cost-effective toolkits for modeling, and are heavily utilized by academics and companies starting to build these capabilities.

Insights generation techniques:

- Data visualization so that insights are recognizable by business users.
- Dashboard creation for tracking promotional impact and key performance indicators.
- Statistical significance testing, to determine if differences are actionable for decisions.
- Presentation creation and delivery to business clients, emphasizing the implications on decision-making.
- This itemization is not exhaustive but should provide a sense of the broad technical skills that data scientists can have. I have seen staff members learn many of these in formal education, and learn others from mentors in a business group. We will provide in-depth examples and case studies applying these skills to sales and marketing environments in later chapters. See Cespedes (2014) for an article on theoretical underpinnings.

3.3.4 Product Development

Initially, most advanced analytics projects are *custom, or bespoke* to a particular client and their own business need. As such, the analyst's methodologies are not standardized, the output format may be uncertain, and there may be several customizations and re-work. This is all expected and in the name of meeting or exceeding a client's expectation.

However, once a group gets positive feedback and senses broad demand for an analytics service, the next phase is to *productize* the solution, which consists of:

- Standardizing the features such as the types of analyses, the dimensions of potential variations, and the form of the output delivery
- Building operational processes enabling production across multiple categories and clients, ultimately driving faster throughput
- Designing quality control processes that can reduce errors and avoid re-work

Product development specialists have the skills to help your group reach this stage, to transition successful ad-hoc projects into sustainable products. Talents of product developers include:

- Designing and documenting procedures in a modular way, rather than "hard coded." This includes detailed comments on the functionality and expected behavior of each procedure. With such a design, the core procedures remain the same, and parameters are passed for each project's specifications.
- Designing databases for scalability to grow as the product deliveries increase, and creating indexes and views for efficiency.
- Agile project management, which includes breaking complex projects into short (usually 2-week) sprints, and prioritizing the inevitable backlog of tasks with respect to business value and complexity measures.
- Integration with other external systems and data sources.
- Creating quality control and unit testing procedures for product components.

In my experience, product development teams are usually multi-disciplinary, because a range of technical and management disciplines are critical. They also can be multi-national, consisting of sub-teams in at least two of: North America, Europe, and Asia concurrently. This distributed geography has advantages of allowing round-the clock development, provided hand-off instructions are daily and well documented. The distributed staff usually brings a benefit of reduced labor fees. The disadvantage of a worldwide distributed product development team is difficulty in scheduling large group meetings, which end up taking place late evening or early morning for at least one group.

3.3.5 Product Management

The product manager role is also focused on productizing analytics solutions, like product development. However, as Figure 3.2 above shows, product managers concentrate on the business strategy, customer needs, and competitive positioning in the marketplace.

Product managers have various skills including market research, customer focus, competitive intelligence, and basic forecasting. In short, they need to develop, own, and update the *business plan* for the product line, current and future.

Note that for big data analytics functions, usually we think of product management as a supplier-side (a.k.a. vendor) responsibility. Indeed, suppliers are selling these productized analytics services to manufacturer/advertiser "client" companies. However, analytics product management is also critical for manufacturer clients that seek to build up innovative, scalable solutions within their companies. During my employment at such large corporations, I have owned data-driven decision support products, and many of the skills articulated here were quite necessary.

I've also grown and led joint product management and product development teams in a variety of big-data analytics firms that were launching and growing product lines such as media planning, targeting, media measurement, and revenue growth (via pricing), amongst others. With that experience, let me enumerate some of the core responsibilities of Product Management that have consistently been critical. You can divide these into two sets: business planning and product ownership.

Business planning functions of product managers are especially critical while new analytics product lines are being prepared for launch. This planning skill also is valuable at the analytics justification stage described in Chapter 2. These include:

- *Market sizing and segmentation*: Determining how many potential customers there are for an analytics product or service, and how to segment these customers. For B to B analytics, possible segmentations could be by company size, department, geography, or industry. For B to C, the segmentation could divide consumer prospects by demographics, occupation, or related interests
- *Competitive landscaping*: Knowing who are the current competitors, or future entrants to this market, along with their market shares and strengths and weaknesses of their products.
- *Stakeholder intelligence*: Utilizing surveys and focus groups of current and prospective buyers plus industry experts. The goal is to understand perceptions of competitors, decision processes of prospective buyers, and unmet needs.
- *Developing product features and functions*: with the above inputs, propose features of a company's analytics solution that will enable favorable comparisons, and fill some of the gaps that stakeholders have identified.

- For big data analytics solutions, examples of features to compete on include: business questions answered, frequency of results delivery, time lag of data, analytical sophistication, delivery method, customer service, and transparency of methodology.

- *Pricing estimates*: suggesting a pricing structure and margin that will cover expenses and encourage rapid trial for new analytics services.

- *Forecasting*: predicting the number of units sold and revenue over time per analytics product line. This will guide planning for future investments. The best forecasts can identify levels of uncertainty, sources of variation, and suggest alternate scenarios and outcomes.

- *Product Ownership*: taking responsibility for the product strategy, and positioning in the marketplace.

- Maintaining and prioritizing the pipeline of product line extensions and innovations over time.

- Contributing to product marketing communications such as press releases, newsletters, and thought leadership at industry trade shows and conferences.

- Training the sales team on messaging for the latest product features, functions, and positioning.

- Gathering feedback from users of the analytics products, as input for product enhancements and improved messaging.

3.3.6 Delivery Specialists

To ensure continual revenue growth from your analytics services, you need to achieve client satisfaction that will lead to renewals. This is especially true for supplier-side companies, and arguably for internal corporate analytics groups. Hence the need for one or more delivery specialists. This role is an operational one, held by a multi-talented individual who has strong project management skills, understands technical product details, is very client focused, and has a high standard for excellence in results. The objective for delivery specialists is to ensure that the big data analytics results are on time, complete, quality checked, insightful, polished, and professional.

Given this cross-disciplinary role description, usually a delivery specialist comes out of another group. This person can be a product developer with strong project management skills. It can be an account manager who has deep product knowledge. Regardless, strong organizational, technical, and communication skills are required.

The delivery specialist especially understands the three core dimensions of an analytics solution, shown in Figure 3.3: quality, time, and cost. A favorite expression I have heard early in my career and adopted in my role as a delivery specialist, is that a solution "cannot be good, fast, and cheap all at once." That is, a solution consists of the specification quality, the timing, and the cost. Once

FIGURE 3.3 Fundamental Dependent Components of an Analytics Solution

this balance is agreed to in a statement of work contract, there cannot be a change in one dimension without affecting the other two.

3.3.7 Account Managers

The account management function is especially critical in service organizations that are selling and delivering big data analytics solutions. This is a single point of contact that can listen to a client's needs, and initiate the crafting of a potential solution. An excellent account manager can serve as an *analytics translator*, which we have discussed in a prior chapter.

The account manager has the critical responsibility of managing expectations before delivery. This includes reminding clients of the agreed upon scope, timing, and format of the solution, and not allowing "scope creep" to enlarge the solution breadth without a change in time or cost.

3.3.8 Business Development

The business development function is responsible for selling analytics products and solutions, and is naturally more critical in a service organization than in a client manufacturer or advertiser firm. More commonly, the role is simply called Sales. An effective big data analytics sales team needs special skills such as identifying unmet customer needs and points of a prospect's dissatisfaction with current solutions. Then, the sales leader must portray the product or solution as an effective alternative to try to meet those needs and soothe the pain points. Importantly, the listening is paramount. Reciting features and benefits of an analytics solution is not effective until you know what the prospect needs.

Note that big data analytics solutions can have a long sales cycle, and an effective business development group must make each touch point further the likelihood of trial. Additionally, there is a skill of adapting the "suggested retail price" from the product management team to a price that the prospect is willing to pay. When no price is acceptable at first, the sales team may pivot to a strategy of free trial usage, so that hands-on experience can accelerate eventual purchase.

Now that we have articulated the core roles of a big data analytics function, let's also point out a few caveats. First, although these roles are distinct, it is important that they not be siloed or separated from each other. An effective company will have close collaboration across the advanced analytics team, and indeed as mentioned above, in smaller companies an individual may hold multiple roles. Second, an individual should not be "pigeon-holed" into just one of these roles for their career. Management must allow an employee's strengths and preferences to change over time. As one scenario, I've seen multiple product managers and delivery specialists shift to business development, once they become enthusiastic with client interaction and show an aptitude for selling.

3.4 Conclusions

In this chapter, we have articulated the different roles required for a complete big data analytics department, ranging from the data-focused positions to client-focused ones. We encourage the reader to apply these descriptions to their own companies or departments. Perhaps this framework can help you identify a way of re-organizing your current small team as you plan future growth. Additionally, these role descriptions can assist as you expand your team with further recruiting.

Alternatively, you may find (especially as years progress post-book release) that this general role taxonomy can be further refined based on the nuances of your own business. If so, feel free to customize per your needs.

3.5 Exercises

1. You are starting a small advanced analytics services company that will serve business clients in the consumer packaged goods industry. You need to start generating revenue within 6 months, and you have funding for a staff of five people.
   a) What are the most important roles you need to fill as you get started?
   b) How can you best allocate your five new hires across those roles?
2. What are some of the key differences between the product development role and the product management role? If you were hiring new staff for each, what qualifications would you look for?
3. How close should the alignment be between the client facing roles of Business Development and Account Management? How should they communicate and collaborate to keep clients satisfied and to increase revenue of your company's advanced analytics practice?
4. How closely should communication be between the Business Development roles and the Product Development and Data Science groups? Is there an organizational risk to have the sales team know too much about "how the sausage is made?"
5. You are a delivery specialist for an analytics services organization, and your business development team has sold an 8-week project for a customer segmentation based on multiple stages in a well-designed product plan. Then unexpectedly the client delays the kickoff meeting 1 week and adds an additional simulation analysis to the project, while stating this must be completed within the 7 weeks remaining. How would you reply, given the fundamental trade-off relationship between quality, time, and cost?

4

LESSONS LEARNED MANAGING BIG DATA DEPARTMENTS

4.1 Differences between Suppliers and Clients

This book is intended for readers across a range of company sizes, structures, and positions within the analytics commercial landscape. Toward that end, I personally have split my big data analytics career to date about evenly between so-called client organizations and supplier companies. At their heart, these are two different types of companies. Client-side companies typically manufacture goods and advertise their product benefits across media channels. These companies generate revenue by selling the products they create, whether foods, beverages, appliances, or financial instruments. Supplier-side firms, by contrast, have a primary objective of selling services (such as big data analytics) to the aforementioned clients. Those services are either sold as fixed-cost projects, software as service licenses, or hourly rate-driven engagements.

Aside from the client-side and supplier-side companies having different core commercial models, what else is distinctive from an advanced analytics perspective? How is the actual day-to-day experience different? From a practitioner perspective, there are benefits to either environment. However, there are also caveats to consider. I will mention a few salient points in the sections that follow.

4.1.1 Client Side Organizations: Critical Points

4.1.1.1 Centrality of Product Teams

At commercially driven client organizations, one perceives the centrality of the products or product lines being sold. Outsiders may refer to the product team

DOI: 10.4324/9780429300363-5

as a "brand team" but in reality, the resources and personnel put against the product take place even before the product is given a brand name. Pharmaceuticals offers a striking example of this, where a generic, molecular name may designate the product and its associated team for years, and then after regulatory approval, the brand name takes over. Nonetheless, I may refer to "product teams" and "brand teams" interchangeably in this chapter.

I have seen across client companies and industries that the product teams are the central organizing construct, whether those products are consumer packaged goods, refrigerators, radiology scanners, or medications. That centrality is justified by the expectation of revenue generation, which becomes reality as the product is launched and sold in the market. There is a core team of product marketers who need to bring the product from early development, through testing, approval, and commercialization.

4.1.1.2 Matrix Organization

Supporting and partnering with the product team is a set of functional departments, consisting of specialists in distinct disciplines with focused training and experience. These specialists include analytics, as well as sales, media, legal and regulatory, operations, technology, and other functions. In fact, these functional specialists work across multiple brand teams.

This construct is called a matrix organization and is illustrated in Figure 4.1. In a matrix organization, each member of an analytics group will be structured along two dimensions:

* the analytical or technical department they belong to, and
* the product teams that they support.

Thus, an extended team meeting for a particular brand will include representatives of all the matrixed functions, for the purposes of raising any technical or regulatory concerns, and for planning critical operational implementation details. Say, for example, one of the big data analytics teams develops and tests a

FIGURE 4.1 Example Matrix Structure for a Commercial Client

predictive model for when a new customer might churn to another brand. This might have been tested within an artificial environment like a historical database with Python code, but now the time has come to discuss production with actual customers. The extended matrixed group meeting is an excellent venue to plan how to roll this out to usage by the consumer call center for production, and address issues like:

- implementing code and other technology for embedding the scoring model within the call center environment,
- writing and approving messaging scripts for operators to use with consumers exceeding the model's churn risk threshold, and
- ensuring that the results pass regulatory concerns, such as ruling out demographic bias.

The benefit of the cross-functional matrix team is having all the relevant perspectives represented for rolling out innovations such as this predictive model.

Say you manage a five-person analytics team, within a client organization of ten or more marketing brands. You therefore must determine how to align your staff to each of these products. The first step as a leader is to understand the needs of each product team based on the lifecycle stage of that product and the marketplace challenges. Here are some examples from an analytics perspective, based on what I have seen over the years:

- One product may be pre-launch, planning for awareness advertising, and needing to develop insightful dashboards regarding product uptake.
- Another product might be facing stiff competition and need to simulate potential customer switching scenarios.
- Yet another product might be wanting to expand from a primary institutional or retail channel and want to "spillover" into more mass-market sales.

As a manager, you need to translate these internal client needs for the different brands into data sets and analytical techniques, and then assign your staff to the teams based on their skills. For an analytics team, the benefit of a matrix organization is development according to brand-driven objectives, and not in an ivory tower vacuum. Then, to help your team grow, internally share project status and the analytics applications to real business problems, for group education of the novel data sources utilized and analytics methodologies.

4.1.1.3 Political Environment

The matrix environment that fosters thorough planning and a range of perspectives can also result in a political environment. Talented employees may have multiple skills and experiences, including those that are nominally aligned to another function in the matrix. When employees discuss their points of view outside of their "swim lanes," defensive and territorial feelings can result. The key for innovation within a corporate environment is to have the group focus less on "who *owns* this part of the solution" and more on efficiently bringing solutions to market and satisfying customers.

4.1.1.4 Satisfaction of Business Impact

Perhaps the most appealing aspect of working for manufacturers is that you can track the impact of your work directly on ultimate sales and customer satisfaction. One can actually witness the customer response and (hopefully) satisfaction upon using the product with your newly embedded analytics algorithm. Additionally, one can truly see whether the analytics-driven process improvements have increased revenue or decreased expenses, and impacted the company's bottom line.

4.1.2 Supplier Side Organizations: Critical Distinctions

When you work on the supplier side, your firm might fall into one of these categories:

- Agency, for advertising, media, or public relations
- Data provider
- Analytics consulting firm
- Management consultant

In my varied career, I have worked for each of these types of companies. They all develop and sell analytics-based solutions to the clients, manufacturers, and advertisers we were previously describing. What do these supplier-side firms have in common, and how are they different in work environments to the clients, especially to practitioners and managers in big data analytics? A few insights follow.

4.1.2.1 Continual Selling

In most provider environments, selling to prospective clients is a continual requirement, especially if your firm's services are funded by clients as short-term projects of 1 year or less. Selling takes two major forms:

1. requests for proposals (RFPs) that describe a firm's capabilities, including advanced analytics

2. pitch presentations, which often include an advanced analytics mini-project performed gratis to show the firm's skills in big data, AI, predictive modeling, etc.

Both of these efforts are usually required for bidding on large, multi-million dollar contracts.

I truly learned the nature of agency life in one supplier role as I prepared for a major analytics delivery presentation for a client. I was focused on how to articulate the quantitative results, associated insights, and operational implications. However, my colleagues the client service and strategy leads were preparing slides on future work that the agency could upsell. I asked them, "is this a delivery meeting or a sales meeting?" The reply was "in this business, you are always selling." Almost 15 years later, I recall those words as a guideline to maintain professionalism and keep ears open for future business opportunities.

4.1.2.2 Time Accounting

For most agencies and consulting firms, employees must bill their hourly time against specific projects, of varying duration. In fact, some analytics groups are judged by *utilization rates* or billability, which is the percentage of time billed that is attributable to client projects. This rate can at minimum be a guideline, but can also be applied as grounds for staff re-allocation or reductions.

Therefore, analytics managers under such circumstances must plan ahead on how to allocate their staff's time between client projects vs. staff training or capabilities building. The frequency of free work provided at pitches (mentioned above) can make such resource planning challenging.

4.1.2.3 Work-Life Imbalance

One consequence of the constant selling environment is the need to work long hours, well into the evenings and weekends. Many supplier-side companies pay analytics managers well, but they maintain lean staffing levels to maintain project margins and profitability. When the additional gratis pitch work inevitably ramps up, one experiences late nights and broken family engagements. During the pandemic era of 2020–2022, marathon sessions in the office decreased, but videoconference meetings from home at off-hours increased.

4.1.2.4 Rapid Innovation

It's important to point out benefits of the supplier side, too. One advantage is that an analytics group can rapidly innovate new solutions. Thomas Edison once said, "necessity is the mother of invention." For agencies and other analytics service providers, the need for selling tends to give rise to packaging and demonstrating new skill sets that give a competitive advantage. One example is the rise of digital analytics in the early 2000s, and social listening sentiment analyses in the late 2000s; at first these were innovative offerings that have now matured into core services.

4.1.2.5 Role Flexibility

Another benefit of supplier-side analytics life is the ability to have a more fluid job description, wear multiple hats, and grow into related disciplines. While I began my career leading big-data analytics groups, I was fortunate in some supplier-side environments to extend experience into campaign operations and product management. Along the way, I self-trained into disciplines like agile product development. Indeed, one growing trend is professionals who transitioned into analytics from non-related university degrees. This flexible environment is a contrast to the more rigid, territorial matrix environment on the client side.

4.2 Performance Management for Big Data Organizations

Once you are fortunate enough to have a larger analytics group, consisting of entry-level individuals through management, you will have to consider career paths for your team. Employees appreciate a work environment where they know what is expected of them, and how to be recognized for advancement. Below we describe a tool that has proven consistently valuable across both client-side and supplier-side analytics-based companies.

4.2.1 The Capabilities Grid Articulates a Career Path

A capabilities grid is a tool for articulating the behaviors that a company expects of its employees at each level of development, roughly at each title. The framework is illustrated in Table 4.1. The rows denote each title level in the department. Several are illustrated as entry level, director, and vice president, but each organization can fill in the rows per its structure. The columns represent distinct, critical skills that are essential for the department's progress. As shown in the table, these are often broken into technical skills and people skills. Technical skills are exemplified by contributions to product development, and capabilities in advanced analytics. People skills include areas such as client management, and collaboration within teams.

The interior cells of the capabilities grid describe the expected performance of colleagues at that professional level related to that skill dimension. As you navigate the column from the first row downward, the performance shows greater responsibility and more significant business impact.

TABLE 4.1 Outline of a Capabilities Grid for an Advanced Analytics Department

Professional Level	Technical Skills		People Skills	
	Product Development	Advanced Analytics	Client Management	Team Collaboration
Entry Level				
...		< Expected Performance, Metrics >		
Director				
...				
Vice President				

Consider, for example, the "Advanced Analytics" section. A progression could read like this:

- *Entry Level*: apply known analytical techniques to one or more projects; show insights and package for client delivery.
- *Director Level*: Manage a team delivering multiple analytics projects to clients; demonstrate the ability to standardize for efficiency and customize per client needs.
- *Vice-President Level*: Manage a group that efficiently delivers a range of analytics-driven solutions for clients. Support launch of multiple company innovations each year.

There is room to adapt the capabilities grid in terms of levels, capabilities, and the expected behaviors, to meet the style of your company. Before finalizing, senior leadership and human resources should approve, and it should be presented to all employees in the department, with allowance for questions, comments, and refinement.

4.2.2 Performance Review Process

Once a capabilities grid is established, then a performance review process becomes quite straightforward. A manager assesses each staff member against each dimension for that person's level and the next level above. The inputs are direct evidence from project work, and inputs from a "360-degree" of colleagues – direct reports, managers, and internal peers within the same department or other groups having frequent collaboration. Client-facing roles may require input from a customer, either directly conveyed or via satisfaction surveys.

There are three primary outcomes that can result:

- If a team member is solidly performing across most dimensions at their current level, then you may consider modest short-term rewards like a raise or bonus if the company has a pool available. However, there is no need to consider promotion at this time. A manager can have a development conversation as to what skills at the next higher level must be developed in the coming year.

- If the employee is exceeding the expectations at the current level across most dimensions, then definitely reward in the short-term, and initiate the internal process for promotion to the next level.
- Finally, if a staffer is not achieving the milestones at their current level across most dimensions, this means there is unlikely to be a short-term incentive. Instead, the situation warrants a serious discussion about what improvements are needed to remain with your department, and perhaps with the company.

4.3 Taking Your Big Data Group to the Next Level

Most of my career roles on the supplier side have had one thing in common: post-startup organizations (or departments) at an inflection point wanting to continue a high growth trajectory. Three of these were agencies seeking to expand their analytics functions with new capabilities and deeper, broader, client relationships. Three of these were data- and product-driven companies wanting to leverage the latest innovations and achieve scale. They all shared some element of applying digital, analytics, and artificial intelligence.

By the end of each journey, my teammates and I had achieved great satisfaction and recognition. Depending on the firm, these rewards were agency of the year, successful product launches, industry recognition, and passing leading competitors in market share. From these experiences, I have learned multiple lessons of what is needed to grow beyond the start-up:

1. Entrepreneurial practices are required, like rolling up your sleeves, wearing many hats, open communication, and periodic late hours. Conventional nine to five roles, staying in swim lanes, do not fly to drive high growth.
2. Frequent demonstrations and capabilities presentations were critical to accelerating growth. Featured were high-tech capabilities, innovative products, and relevant case studies. The experience always had to be forefront, showing that "we have done this many times and you can rest assured with us."
3. Most importantly, operational discipline was key, and necessary. Across all of these experiences, I encouraged my teams to implement sorely needed protocols like:
   - Meeting agendas and follow-ups with written action items, owners, and deadlines.
   - Quality control procedures to ensure scalability and accurate delivery, before reaching the client.
   - Knowledge sharing across the department, so that staff members learned from peers, feeling empowered to share and borrow best practices.

- Standardization and documentation of core processes, including client proposals, capabilities meetings, and product methodology explanations.
- Customer focus on key accounts, tracked regularly by activities and financials. This has minimized distractions taking away from our precious time.

Some of these operational enhancements may seem obvious. However, a start-up company or department might ignore these as they struggle to gain a toe-hold in their category. I have learned that to move on to the next level of growth, these disciplinary tactics can make a tremendous difference.

The lessons above are described in terms of supplier-side companies. However, often client-side manufacturers create new "centers of excellence" in areas like advanced analytics, machine learning, media, or customer relationship management. The employees in these new department, while matrixed, still have latitude to rapidly expand with success. Therefore, these lessons can also apply to client-side innovation teams.

4.4 Conclusions

In this chapter, we discussed organizational design for client-side and supplier-side analytics departments. There are distinctions in terms of clarity of structure, fluidity of role, and the expectations of business development

We closed, however, with two unifying frameworks: the capabilities grid for articulating team expectations and tracking performance, and the lessons learned to bring an advanced analytics organization to the next level. We encourage the reader to apply and customize these constructs for their own companies or departments.

4.5 Exercises

1. As an employee, which of the core differences between client-side and supplier-side analytics environments that are spelled out in this chapter most resonate with you? How might they affect your decision to work within one area vs. the other?
2. Consider how you would apply the capabilities grid to your own analytics team. If just starting out, then think about the group you aim to have in 2 years time. How many levels of capabilities would there be? What are the core skill dimensions to measure?
3. What methods have you seen a company employ to encourage entrepreneurship and yet still respect work-life balance? This can be a difficult balance to strike in managing an analytics-driven innovative team to get to the next level.

PART II
Analytics Business Applications

5

SEGMENTATION

Categorizing Your Customers

The next few chapters of this textbook describe business applications of big data analytics, articulating both methodology and lessons learned from project implementations. We start with customer segmentation, which is probably one of the earliest applications of big data analytics.

5.1 Motivation for Segmentation

I've implemented and overseen customer segmentation projects applied across financial services, telecommunications, healthcare, packaged goods, and other industries. Within each industry, you can further subdivide applications into consumer and business segmentation.

From a business standpoint, segmentations are ways of dividing your customer database into groups for further actionability. The number of groups may be fairly small (say two to five) or may number in the thousands.

As illustrated in Figure 5.1, the groups are created based on:

*   attributes of each customer,
*   previous promotions that customer has seen (for your product, and perhaps competitors), and
*   each customer's behaviors (such as purchase history, interactions with your ecosystem, and payment patterns).

DOI: 10.4324/9780429300363-7

The business value of creating these groups is the ability to take segment-specific actions in the future, including:

- customized messaging or creative in communications,
- specific account policies (e.g. credit line, length of service) (see Haimowitz et al. 1997), and
- tailored promotional terms (e.g. offers, discounts).

Underlying this framework are certain business principles and assumptions:

- *Predictiveness*: if customers have exhibited certain prior behaviors, then one can predict how they can behave in the near future, after a promotional or policy action.
- *Aggregation*: For some reason, the business needs to take business action at the group level, rather than solely at the individual level. This may be due to:
  - preservation of customer privacy, or
  - operational limitations, on the number of differentiated promotions of communications that can be produced.
- *Relevance*: There is a belief that the messaging or promotional choices made to all customers in a segment will be relevant to (nearly) all members of that segment and resonate enough to prompt desirable action.

Here are two examples of marketing actions driven by a customer segmentation:

1. When launching a new product, a company develops prioritized offers for prospects that have been previous *early adopters* of other new products recently appearing in the category. The offer calls out innovative product features. The offer calls out innovative product features.
2. Communication to a *younger segment* of newly acquired customers is conducted exclusively with mobile apps, offering convenience, chatbot support, and a social community of other customers to share experiences.

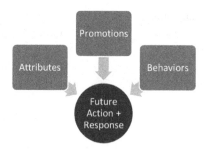

FIGURE 5.1 Conceptual Framework for Segmentation

However, a business must be careful when performing segmentation not to engage in a type of simplistic stereotyping that can lead to discrimination, whether intentional or otherwise.

Now that we have summarized the main reasons why companies create customer segmentations, let's proceed by first formalizing the definition of a segmentation, and specifying the underlying data structure required for segmentation. Then we can describe how different big data analytical methods are utilized to create actionable segmentations.

5.2 Segmentation Defined: Probabilistic vs. Partition

Say you have an (active) database of n customers and you want to divide them into k groups (k may or may not be known ahead of time). A segmentation is an assignment that maps

Customers $C_1, C_2, ..., C_n$

to

Segments $S_1, S_2, ... S_k$ by denoting

Probabilities $P_{j1}, P_{j2}, ..., P_{jk}$ of a Customer j belonging to each of the k segments,

where the probabilities P_{ji} add up to 1.

Note that there can be more than one segmentation relevant to a project. In pharmaceutical marketing, for example, segments may be assigned to the same physicians such as high decile prescriber, specialist, key opinion leader, and promotion responsive. This demonstrates a need for separate segmentation schemes in the same project, each of with a separate set of segments S_i.

The above specifies a situation where a customer may be partially assigned with probabilities to multiple segments. This is the more analytically and mathematically general version, but not often used in business. More commonly, there is a unique assignment of each customer to one and only one segment, also referred to as a *partition* of customers to the segments. Mathematically, that means one of the $P_{j'k} = 1$, and all other $P_{jk} = 0$.

However, in this chapter, we will maintain the option of the more general case of segmentation, as it showcases how big data analytics methods can be applied.

5.3 Data Preparation to Support Segmentation

A segmentation project requires as a first phase a particular data preparation that is amenable to analysis, which is demonstrated in Table 5.1. This table shows a general structure that can become much more detailed in actual business cases.

The table is denormalized, aggregated, and summarized at the customer level. In order to create this table, joins must be executed with the Customer ID as the primary key, linking:

TABLE 5.1 Denormalized Table Structure for Segmentation Analyses

Customer ID	Demographics			External Attributes		Account Parameters		Summarized Behaviors	
	Age	Gender...		Exercise Level	Social Media Active.	Line	Interest Rate	Total Purchase	Avg Time to Pay
AB1234									
AC3457									
....									

- one or more customer dimension tables and
- one or more transactional fact tables of customer behaviors.

The table for analysis consists of several sets of fields:

- The customer ID itself, which is distinct for each row
- A set of customer demographics that can be either self-reported or gathered from some external data source
  - For consumer segmentations, examples are age, gender, ethnicity, household income, and presence of children.
  - For commercial segmentations, examples may be size of the company, years in business, industry code, and annual revenue.
- External attributes may be available if acquired from additional data sources. They can be self-reported by the customer on surveys, or matched from an external provider. Examples are media channel preferences, lifestyle and hobby preferences, or other fields relevant to your product lines.
- Account parameters describe the terms of how you maintain business with that customer, including terms of business, promotional frequency, etc.
- Summarized behaviors aggregate the transactions for which that customer has performed with respect to your business. These may be averages, totals, counts, or extremes, and they may be over a time period of your choosing. However, they should be consistently applied across customers in the segmentation analysis.

Table 5.1 illustrates a partial view of a consumer segmentation table for a credit card marketing application. The account parameters include the credit line and the interest rate for that customer, and the summarized behaviors indicate financial performance such as total purchase levels and average time to pay the monthly credit bill. As mentioned above, there can be far more additional detail in the analysis table, and it can be customized for the resulting planned actions.

5.4 Analytical Segmentation Methods

There are various analytics methods that can be applied to create data-driven customer segmentations. We describe them below and offer examples for each:

- Categorization: choosing specific values for categorical variables can create a basic segmentation which may be appropriate for customized creative or messaging. Examples come from demographics, as shown in Table 5.2, which divides households into three categories to determine the creative message to send in a prospecting solicitation for a new financial service (such as insurance or credit cards).

There are 18 segments articulated, each based on a combination of categorical values of household-level demographics that should be readily available in the customer database. Thus, a young family with children in an urban address might get sent a creative featuring a city playground near traffic-filled streets that says "Life can be complicated." Furthermore, the message would likely be sent on digital channels like mobile ads, text messages, or email.

- *Thresholding*: This segmentation technique is based on setting levels of one or more customer-level numerical behavioral outcomes. For example, customers can be assigned into quintiles based on total purchase volume over the past 12 months, with 20% of the customers falling into each quintile.
- *Behavioral Clustering*: This multivariate technique employs combinations of quantitative behavior variables to create groups utilizing similarity scores based on a distance metric. Let's come back to the credit card example that we introduced in Section 5.1. We wish to divide up to millions of consumers in the credit card portfolio based on their purchasing behavior and payment patterns. A three-dimensional cluster analysis could be developed using these variables: total sales line utilization, and frequency of late

TABLE 5.2 Demographic Category-Based Segmentation for Creative Messaging

| Age (Head of HH) | Presence of Children | Geography | | |
		Rural	Suburban	Urban
18–44	Yes			
	No			
45–64	Yes	*<18 demographic segments>*		
	No			
65 Plus	Yes			
	No			

payments. As we will cover below, it is important to have these dimensions be uncorrelated and all at the same scale (such as 0 to 1).

- Thus, each consumer is represented with a triple of zero-to-one variables of (Sales level, Lateness, and Utilization). A high-spending customer that uses most of their line and pays promptly would have a triple like (0.9, 0.9, 0.05) and a moderate-spending customer with a high credit line who is often late would have a triple like (0.5, 0.2, 0.9).
- Each customer can be thought of as a three-dimensional point in the Cartesian space of Figure 5.2. A distance metric such as Pythagorean distance can be used to aggregate customers who are close together in the space, and thus behave similarly with their credit cards. We shall go into more details of this clustering approach in the next section.

- *Predictive Models*: A predictive model is a functional form that is fit from a training set of data and then is applied to a holdout sample for validation. The purpose is to predict a behavioral outcome. Staying with the credit card example of this section, a marketing team may want to develop a predictive model of "estimated future 12 months spend on credit card." Alternatively, a risk analyst may want to develop a similar model to predict "likelihood of not paying the minimum balance within the next 6 months."
  - More generally stated, the inputs for the predictive model can be the demographics, external attributes, and account parameters of Table 5.1, and the output can be one of the behavioral outcome variables.
  - Clearly predictive modeling is a big data analytics project. In fact, we will dedicate an entire chapter to predictive modeling in this book. However, why is a predictive model a form of segmentation? Simply because the predicted values can be used for a segmentation scheme, of

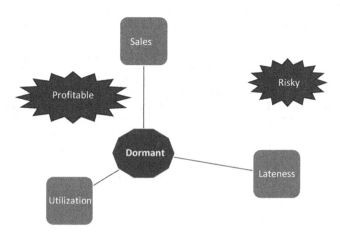

FIGURE 5.2 Three-Dimensional Behavioral Clustering, Credit Card Example

the thresholding variety stated above. One example is how differentiated credit policies and communications are given to consumers with
different threshold tiers of credit scores, which are in turn a predictive
model of reliable payment, on a scale of 0 to 800.

- *Hybrid Segmentation*: Segments are often defined that are combinations of
the above frameworks. For example, a certain seasonal or holiday promotion can be sent to the segment that are both high spenders, and low credit
risk, combined with the appropriate demographic categorization: Female
in household and presence of children for Mother's Day, or presence of
teenagers for graduation gift promotions.

5.5 Technical Details to Focus on for Meaningful Business Segmentations

In order for a segmentation to be insightful and actional within business, it is
important to note the following technical guidelines that underlie the analytics
methodology. In particular, let's revisit the variables in the summarized Table
5.1 and focus on the clustering approach we've illustrated in Figure 5.1. Clustering relies on a set of observations and a distance metric and is most often
accomplished either with:

a. "bottom up" agglomerative method that groups N observations based on
distances and grows the clusters incrementally. The run time is a worst-
case order N-squared approach, and number of clusters is data-driven.
b. "top-down" K-means, or nearest neighbor approach that specifies the
number of clusters K, initiates with centroids, and assigns points to the K
clusters based on closest distance, and runs in order N time.

More details on specifics of clustering can be found in the data mining textbooks (Duda et al. 2001 or Provost and Fawcett 2013).

5.5.1 Segmentation Objectives Tied to Analytics Constraints

With either solution, the objective of clustering for business segmentation is
to produce groups of customers or prospects that are similar in meaningful
and actional attributes and behaviors. Additionally, the distinct clusters should
differ from each other in important enough ways to warrant different communications, offers, or account policies. To achieve this, there are some technical
factors to keep in mind as the clusters are being produced, itemized below.

- *Independence*: The fields entered into the clustering algorithm should have
a minimal relationship. If not completely independent, then nearly so,
meaning the correlation between the variables is close to zero. Stated more

precisely, the J input fields to the clustering algorithm should form J orthogonal dimensions, to as close as the extent possible. This is important
so that each attribute or behavior measured represents a distinct aspect of
the customers being segmented, and no particular dimension gains undue
attention.

- An example of dependent input variables would be behavioral attributes
  like *number of purchases* and *total spend*. These are dependent because additional purchases naturally imply more spending. A pair that is more independent would be *number of purchases* and *spend per purchase*, as one captures
  frequency, and the other captures volume. Other examples from lifestyle
  variables are *frequency of exercise* and *self-reported fitness*. These are likely to
  be correlated, and so a segmentation modeler should either choose one of
  these, or combine to a blended factor, as we will discuss below.
- *Consistent scale*: The input variables should appear at the same scale, so that
  the distance metrics comparing two points do not overweight any particular dimension. As exemplified in Table 5.1, total spend may have a range
  from zero to tens of thousands of dollars, while social media activity level
  may be on a 1 to 10 scale.
  - To reduce this variation of scale, consider standardizing the partic-
    ularly large variables by dividing the maximum observed value, or
    an estimated maximum potential value. Then the numbers like total
    spend would reduce to a 0 to 1 scale. Another option I've used is taking
    a logarithm of the numerical value, which reduces scale dramatically.
- *Filtering of Outliers*: One should remove isolated customers whose values
  across one or more dimensions are far outside the population ranges in
  your database. The risk is that they will be erroneously attached to another
  cluster, where they might distort the distribution, and summary statistics
  (e.g. average values). It may be a better business policy to handle such outliers as exceptions handled by threshold-related business rules.

5.5.2 Step by Step Segmentation Procedure

In order to maintain each of the above criteria for a commercially actionable
segmentation, below is a cluster-based segmentation sequence that I have found
successful across multiple jobs, industries, and applications:

1. Pre-analysis data engineering:
   - Aggregate and join disparate customer data sources to produce a de-
     normalized table of one record per customer with key demographic,
     attitudinal, and behavioral attributes, as shown in Table 5.1.
2. Remove outliers:
   - Filter out observations with extreme outliers across one or more dimen-
     sions. Outliers can be defined as more than three standard deviations
     from the mean value.

3. Standardization:
   - Convert variables as needed to a standardized order of magnitude, as mentioned in the prior section. Zero to one is a popular choice.
4. Convert low-order categorical variables to numeric for clustering:
   - While other segmentation techniques (decision trees, selection business rules, etc.) can utilize categorical variables, clustering requires numeric fields. Thus low-cardinality categories can have individual values represented as a zero or one flag, such as "customer is college educated." Some call these "dummy variables." However, this is discouraged for high cardinality categorical variables – it is better to save those variables, if critical to segmentation, for dividing customers either before or after the clustering.
5. Dimensionality reduction
   - This is a significant step that removes correlated variables and aims to make your input dimensions nearly orthogonal, a critical criterion for successful clustering. Two main methods have proven successful:
     - i.) Plot pairwise correlation coefficients of all standardized numerical input variables. Choose among those that are highly correlated, meaning absolute value of greater than or equal to 0.6.
     - ii.) Perform a *principal components analysis* that will produce a subset of variables that are linear combinations of the input variables and by calculation are orthogonal. This step will require interpreting the principal components for meaning. In the examples we have been discussing, components could have interpretations like "heath conscious" or "digitally savvy." The technique is found in most statistical packages like SAS, R, and Python, and is explained well in Han and Kamber (2006).
6. Determine the likely number of clusters
   - One may not know in advance how many clusters there are, meaning how many fundamentally different types of customers exist. As a first guess, you can choose "low" or "high" for each dimension, but that results in exponential growth in segments, and many combinations may be blank.
   - A way to estimate is take a random sample of your data, say 2–5%, and perform an agglomerative clustering with a standard distance metric. The sample is for efficiency. One can view a dendrogram and scatterplots of key dimensions to say at what count of segments is the distribution desirable: minimal tiny clusters, centers consistent with one's business expectations. Repeat more than once with a different random sample of customer data, to confirm the cluster count.
7. Estimate centroids and cluster with K means
   - Once the count of segments has been determined, perform K means clustering with centroid estimates for each cluster, as observed in distributions from the prior step.

- Note that several statistical packages have a version of K means clustering that detects or recommends an optimal clustering number. In effect, this combines this step and the prior one. However, I have found that regardless, a manual review of alternative cluster counts helps with accountability of the results.

8. Review distributions for each cluster
   - Importantly, calculate and review the distributions of customer counts per cluster, and inspect the statistical distribution of key business-focused variables for each segment. Make sure the standard divisions of core factors are not too wide per segment.

9. Describe each segment
   - Leverage your business understanding, and consider whether segments appear to exhibit distinct behaviors, lifestyles, and attitudes that you would recognize. Are these segments consistent with your incoming hypotheses or other market research? There should be few pure surprises.
   - As a "litmus test" for whether the clusters are acceptable, assign a name and write a short description for each. Ultimately, this will be required in your presentations to stakeholders in operational implementations.
   - Here is one example from a financial services credit card space: "New Generation Frequent but Prompt" shown in the cluster output as young, digitally savvy customers who use the card frequently, with low spending levels, and pay promptly.

10. Integrate cluster results to full database
    - Once a cluster code is assigned to each customer ID, match that segment code back to the original customer-level data sets, for further insights we will describe this in the next section.

5.6 Making Your Segmentation Actionable

One gains a sense of pride and satisfaction completing a segmentation analysis where the customer groups are distinctive and consistent with industry parameters. However, in the business world success cannot stop there: it is important to get your segmentation utilized and not just "sit on the shelf." In this section, we itemize approaches to bring that impact, either within your firm or for your clients.

5.6.1 Extracting Segment Insights

The first step is to summarize and extract segment-specific insights for your different stakeholders such as sales, marketing, media, or operations. Here is where you can leverage the full range of customer variables that are now supplemented with the segment identifier. Below are examples of how to characterize the insights, by answering straightforward questions.

- *Profiles and Personas*: Here you answer *Who* the customers are in each segment. Utilize the mean and distributions of all matched variables to profile the customers in that segment. Start by providing a name, short description, and an in-depth analysis of the demographics, lifestyles, and attitudes that segment. All of these can be used to create a persona of that segment's personality, characteristics, and beliefs, that can dictate the most relevant messaging and creative elements.
- *Purchase and Payment Summaries*: These summarized transactional behaviors at the segment level can answer *What* are the behaviors this segment has in the market. What is the level of consumption with the market category, your brand, and competitors? For example, is this segment a high category purchase segment that has yet to try your brand, or alternatively, a moderate category purchase segment where your brand has a strong market share.
- Equally important is identification of segments that have sub-optimal behaviors, either by being too expensive to maintain, or even introducing risk from financial exposure or delinquencies that lead to write offs. Quantifying an argument to reduce spend on such customers, or write them off, is often well-received, for it allows more productive use of investment on profitable segments.
- Also included in this behavioral assessment is *promotion and incentive responsiveness*. Do customers in this segment respond to frequent ad impressions, emails, or sales calls? Do they respond to samples, discounts, lower interest rates, or additional credit lines?
    - In one retail financial services study, Haimowitz and Schwartz (1997) performed a cluster-based segmentation and demonstrated clearly different purchase and payment behaviors between segments and determined an optimal credit line for each segment that maximized net present value for the retailer issuing the credit cards.
- *Channel Preferences*: This answers *How* to reach customers who are in this segment, by understanding the media channels that segment prefers. Do they view television on traditional TV sets with a cable package, or with internet-based TV on a mobile device? Do they respond to emails with opens and click-throughs? Are they active on social media? Do in-person field force visits drive increased brand trial? These channel preferences may come from your own transactional data, from predictive models, or from externally sourced customer-level attribute data. The source may determine your confidence in this information.
- Segment-specific channel preferences allow a brand and its media agency to select the optimal media strategy and tactics for reaching customers and prospects for that segment. Combined with the creative suggestions, these

can combine to recommend a *next best action* of how to communicate with customers in that segment.

- *Salient Segment Differences*: Critical for segmentation projects is describing how the segments differ from each other, for that can dictate the resources required for activation in market. Are the segments distinct enough to warrant different creative, messaging, materials, and channel plans? These can each require development and labor costs. Or is such special treatment only required for one or two segments? As an analytics leader, be prepared to justify differences if warranted to gain incremental response from custom treatment.

5.6.2 Segment-Specific Activation

A primary reason for conducting a marketing segmentation is to *activate*, sending customized messages across ideal channels with tailored offers based on a combination of segment-based and personalized factors.

If the segmentation was conducted with current customers who have provided permission and their contact information, then activation can be straightforward. Utilize the favorable channels where information is provided and send messages that encourage either further product adoption or loyalty. I have conducted such personalized messaging in retail packaged goods as well as healthcare and demonstrated that customized communications deliver a significant revenue lift over generic messaging.

However, often a segmentation is conducted with the intent of recruiting new customers. In such cases, one is trying to reach prospects without prior transactional history and often without contact information. In this case, big data analytics is again critical, in developing a predictive model for desirable segments.

Two common examples:

- In financial services, credit offers sent to consumers based on a credit score model, which have likelihood of paying without default.
- In healthcare marketing, programmatic targeting models that serve ads anonymously to digital devices or TV households based on a privacy-safe prediction that the recipient is likely to have a specific medical condition.

We will cover more specifics on predictive models for prospecting in later chapters of this book.

5.7 Conclusions

In this chapter, we dove deeply into customer segmentation as a core business application of data science and analytics. We stepped through a start to finish process, including necessary data engineering, analytical techniques, and critical guidelines for making the results statistically valid. We concluded with lessons learned on how to make the segmentation insightful, and actionable for sales, marketing, and operations functions. Ultimately, the segments should be distinctive and explainable and warrant strong consideration for taking action, which will drive incremental revenue or cost efficiencies.

5.6 Exercises

1. Describe a segmentation often used in your industry for marketing or sales prospecting, or for establishing a new customer relationship. How are the segments quantified: based on demographics, attributes, behaviors, or a combination? Define two of the segments precisely and call out the attributes or behaviors utilized.
2. You find your customer database has critical fields at differing orders of magnitude: total spend ranges from 0 to $10,000 duration of account from 0 to 3 years, and days to pay bill from 0 to 45. How can you process these fields to make them usable for segmentation.
3. Your consumer data asset has over 50 media channel attributes on a scale of 1 (low) to 10 (high) with either surveyed or modeled preferences. Examples are "responsiveness to emails," "active social media user," and "watching TV on a mobile device." Some attributes list specific channels by name.
   a) Which of these attributes are potentially highly correlated with each other?
   b) How would you test your hypotheses?
   c) If you discover correlations, how would you handle these 50 attributes for use in a customer segmentation?
4. In your business domain, describe a channel activation that can accept a segmentation output file with an account identifier and segment descriptor, and implement alternative communications or business policies.
   a) What operational systems are involved?
   b) How can you track performance once the segments are so deployed?

6

TARGETING

Getting It "Right"

6.1 An Expansive View of Targeting

Targeting is a core element of Marketing and Sales functions across industries. This is what enables the efficient allocation of financial, personnel, and media resources to achieve a profitable result. When speaking with Marketing and Sales Vice-Presidents across industries and decades, remarkably many of them have mentioned a variant on this phrase:

Targeting is reaching the right prospect with the right message at the right channel and the right time.

What is particularly noteworthy about this statement is that targeting is ascribed more than merely selecting the right individuals to promote to, but also the execution of what message is given, and the time and "location" of that message.

Some companies are so passionate about this mantra that they abbreviate this objective as "R4." The question begs, what exactly is meant by "right" when it comes to targeting. We will first get more specific by clarifying the business objectives of each "right," and then demonstrate with two business applications just how data mining can help fulfill the more precise targeting needs

Returning to our R4 catch phrase, we need closer precision before we can utilize our massive data stores for accurate targeting. Thus,

- *The right prospect*: this refers to someone who is likely to be in the market for a product or service in the same category as yours. This may be due to known prior purchase history, or the similarity to others who have already purchased from you. For criticality of precise data, see Sylvester and Spaeth (2019).

DOI: 10.4324/9780429300363-8

- *The right message*: this is a message that would increase the likelihood that the prospect would consider your product especially.
- *The right place*: this could refer to a physical "place" that situates the prospect near a transaction, or it could be another type of marketplace, such as an online catalog. Alternatively, this place could be a media channel where prospects get educated about the options in a category.
  - A competing point of view might say "right place" in this context includes the cost as much or more than the location. If the right prospect who is already interested in your category can be found cost effectively in any location, then that is sufficient; the location itself need not move the prospect along the purchase path.
- *The right time*: this refers to a time when the prospect is actively considering a transaction that could include your product or service. The targeting too early will at best be a notification of an eventual need in the future where your message may be forgotten. The targeting too late can mean your prospect has already converted to a competitor in your space.

6.2 Targeting Examples in Sales and Marketing

Now as promised, we will consider two applied examples of targeting found in distinct industries, and the implications of the "R4" objectives.

1. Targeting professional prospects and customers to support a field sales force.
2. Targeting consumers for digital media advertising.

These examples are divergent enough that together they can illustrate the various factors to consider in developing a successful targeting program.

6.2.1 Sales Force Targeting

Many industries use personal sales forces, including investments, pharmaceuticals, medical devices, and computer software. Figure 6.1 illustrates that a salesperson is assigned a particular geographic territory, and must choose among dozens or hundreds of professionals to call on, in person according to available schedules and willingness of the clients to meet with salespeople.

FIGURE 6.1   Salespeople Must Prioritize among Clients in Their Territory Adapting Messages and Channels

However, not all clients are equally important to visit, not should even the priority prospects get the same frequency of visits. That is where the targeting comes in, and requires big data analytics that summarizes various customer data.

Salespeople are usually given lists of leads, personal or corporate prospects with supporting data: contact information, prior product experience, and often a *segment* describing prior product experience. See Table 6.1 which shows a section of a targeting list for a hypothetical sales representative, who has in her product mix a cardiovascular-related product.

Depending on industry and country regulations, certain levels of customer-level information may be available. The items in this table may come from approved third-party data providers. Alternatively, they may be gathered through surveys conducted with customer permission. Consequently, there may be a mix of numeric and categorical information.

In this case and given such data, what does our "R4" targeting imperative mean for the prospects on the list of a salesperson, given their bag of products they are selling? How does Big Data factor into meeting the R4 objective?

In the cases of professional sales teams, they are establishing a relationship, and visiting their clients on a regular basis. For this reason, another framework used to describe this targeting scenario is *Next Best Action* (alternatively called *Next Best Engagement).* Next Best Action includes whom to target, when to communicate, what message should to provide, and over what channel to correspond. The channel selection, in particular, has grown in relevance with the Covid pandemic restricting in-person visits, and the widespread adoption of viable alternate channels like videoconferencing, emails, webinars, and professional social networks

Big Data analytics can provide multiple solutions for such business-to-business targeting and next best action challenges. This becomes apparent as you quantitatively express the core decisions:

1. Which prospect has the highest expected future usage of my brand?
2. Which channel provides the greatest expected lift from each prospect?
3. What messaging content and creative most resonate with this prospect?

TABLE 6.1 Sample Section of a Salesperson Contact List

Prospect Name	Specialty	Segment	Address and Contact Info.	Category Usage	My Product Usage
Dr. A	Primary	Pre-Trial	<hidden>	Low	None
Dr. B	Specialist	Trial	<hidden>	High	Low
Dr. C	Primary	Loyalist	<hidden>	Medium	High

Once you have answers to these questions, you can select the expected most valuable prospects, and communicate with each on the most impactful and profitable channels using the messaging and creative that resonates individually. Aside from tie-breaking business rules, and orchestration among deployment channels, solving these questions can provide substantive answers toward targeting these professionals. Now, let's investigate the details behind each of these questions:

1. Expected future brand usage by prospect: Note some call this estimation *headroom modeling,* since it sets a realistic ceiling on the customer's potential. In practice, I have seen one simplistic version: presume the entire category goes to your brand, which is too optimistic. Another option for low-performing brands is to presume that brand can reach the estimated market share of the entire customer database. That is more realistic, but fails for high performers and may ignore systematic issues with low performers.

   More reasonable than these "rules of thumb" approaches is to develop a combination of predictive models combined with heuristic business rules. The first step in a predictive model is to see if the prospect or customer can be assigned to a segment, as discussed in our prior chapter. Then create a market share model based on historical training data of customers you feel are at an appropriate market share and fairly frequently promoted. Additional adjustment factors can be employed to the model results, to account for structural roadblocks or special opportunities.

2. Channel-specific predictive response models can similarly be built from training data on each prospect if data allows, or otherwise by finding a segment of similar profressionals. For example, modeling how each prospect's behavior changes with increasing frequency by channel, holding all else constant. A prototypical curve appears in Figure 6.2, where the horizontal

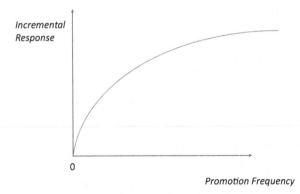

FIGURE 6.2 Frequency response curve for channel frequency and incremental behavior

axis is frequency and the vertical axis is incremental usage over baseline levels.

3. In terms of messaging content and creative, those solutions are usually best tested with either a design of experiments analysis using a setup where multiple varying creative elements are attempted. Alternatively, one can in a data-driven way evaluate the attributes of the prospect or customer to expected messaging response, using a cross-tab analysis or a decision tree related model.

6.2.2 Digital Consumer Targeting

Each day in the US, major brands will serve millions of digital ads to consumers across formats and channels, including display, online video, email, paid search and audio. The ads are served to consumers based on inferred interest or purchase history. The inferences are usually based on data-driven segments built with underlying predictive models.

As an example, consider a medical device company that sells products that assist Type 2 Diabetes patients, such as glucose monitors, exercise step counters, or medication reminders. They serve digital display advertising to consumers for a new product launch, and two of the media placements are illustrated in Figure 6.3.

On the left placement, two banner ads for the medical device product are placed on the condition page of an endemic health publisher's website. The ads are shown to a random 20% of the visitors that come to that page, since five brands have contracted for that space. The inference is that visitors to this web page are self-selecting as interested in Type 2 Diabetes information, and thus may be patients, relatives, or caregivers of patients.

On the right placement, two banner ads for the same product are served while a consumer is checking their messages on a leading email website portal.

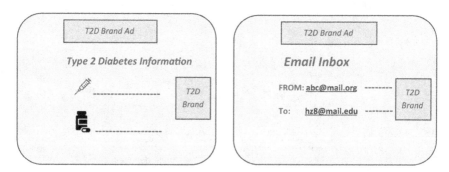

FIGURE 6.3 Display Consumer Advertising: Via Endemic Healthcare Websites or on Programmatic Ad Serving

The ads are served only if the digital device of the consumer belongs to a data segment that suggests a high likelihood of a Type 2 diabetes patient.

What does the "right" targeting language mean in this consumer digital use case?

- *Right prospect*: Consumers viewing the digital ads should be either diagnosed with the disease that this medical device assists, in this case Type 2 diabetes, or otherwise be interested in a potential glucose monitor purchase.
- *Right message*: The message should describe one or more core product features that will make an exposed consumer want to find out more. For a naïve or new to category consumer, the message should provide some education or assurance. For an experienced category user, emphasis on a favorable feature that competitors do not have.
- *Right place*: The ad should be served in a context where it will be noticed and resonate, or ideally where the consumer would read the information.
- *Right time*: The ad should be served at a time when a consumer is open to learning more about this device.

Comparing the two options above of serving this display ad, the endemic page condition placement exceeds the programmatic placement in the email browser on the right place and right time categories. However, as we shall see, other factors must be considered among these two options, like volume of reach, and cost to serve the impressions.

6.3 Measuring the Success of Targeting

When running a promotional campaign to either consumers or professionals, you will have specific target segments in mind that you are trying to reach. Using media terms, the people reached via your campaign are the *audience,* and those people in your target are known as a *qualified audience.* Since there may be multiple target segments, there are correspondingly multiple ways for an audience to be qualified. Consider the consumer targeting example from the prior section. The medical device company may have a demographic-based target of U.S. males aged 50 and older, due to the objectives and messaging of the campaign. Alternatively, they may also have a medically based target in mind, and wish to reach patients who are likely diagnosed with Type 2 diabetes.

Additionally, a targeted media campaign can be served concurrently to multiple media sources, as the two illustrated in Figure 6.3. In current practice, consumer digital health campaigns may have five to ten or more distinct media sources where ads are placed, and even then, a media source can be further subdivided by device type (desktop vs mobile vs. tablet), or other criteria. With this variety, a marketer needs to make decisions as to where to invest their media budget across channels, sub-channels, and specific tactics.

For that reason, and given the specification of a qualified audience, we can define several related criteria of successful targeting:

1. Percent of people reached that are qualified
2. Volume of qualified audience reached
3. Cost efficiency of qualified reach, or cost per qualified person reached.

Let's consider again the example from Figure 6.3 comparing two media sources. Say we have this data (Table 6.2):

The targeting metrics for the endemic website are as follows:

- 20% qualified audience (per the table)
- 1,500,000 consumers reached (note the frequency of two), and thus 300,000 qualified consumers reached.
- The media cost is $120,000 ($40 per thousand impressions and 3 million impressions served), which makes the cost per qualified consumer is $0.40.

For the programmatic media, using similar calculations to get these metrics

- 18% qualified audience (per the table)
- 2,000,000 consumers reached (note the frequency of five) and thus 360,000 qualified consumers reached
- The media cost is $120,000 here as well, which makes the cost per qualified consumer at $0.33

Interestingly, in this hypothetical case, the endemic site reaches a higher rate of qualified audience, but the programmatic has a higher volume of qualified consumers and a lower cost per qualified individual.

This realistic example is one reason why programmatic digital advertising has risen so dramatically; targeting quality rates have improved significantly, and the cost has remained quite low due to automation through automated ad exchanges and real-time bidding.

One extra thought is to compare the qualified reach percentage to a benchmark, to better understand how well they are targeting. In the diabetes glucose

TABLE 6.2 Comparing Two Consumer Digital Media Channels within a Campaign

	Endemic Website	Programmatic Advertising
Impressions served	3,000,000	10,000,000
Cost per thousand impressions (CPM)	$40.00	$12.00
Average frequency per reached consumer	2.0	5.0
Audience quality percentage	20%	18%

meter example, say national statistics show the U.S. prevalence of type two diabetes is 11%. Taking that as a baseline, one could say the healthcare endemic website has a targeting index of 100 ⋆ (20% divided by 11%) or 182. Similarly, the programmatic advertising has a targeting index of 100⋆ (18% divided by 11%) or 164.

What we have thus far glossed over is: how do you know whether or not your promotional campaign is actually reaching a target audience? That comes down to data collection. In the case of the personal B to B promotion, one can collect field force call data of which clients were visited. In the case of consumer advertising, one can introduce online surveys, or match media exposure records (through tagging) to "offline" transactional records to know if the reached consumers fit the target segment criteria. We will explain this latter method in more depth, in our chapter on Data Privacy.

6.4 Fundamental Trade-Off between Precision and Privacy[1]

In this section, we present a framework especially appropriate to the U.S. pharmaceutical direct-to-consumer (DTC) advertising marketplace. However, the targeting trade-offs presented here are also relevant to other industries where maintaining consumer privacy is critical.

As background, pharmaceutical direct-to-consumer (DTC) advertising has risen in recent decades. We show trends from the pre-pandemic era. From 1997 to 2016, as summarized in JAMA, spending on DTC marketing climbed from $2 Billion or 12% of total marketing to almost $10 Billion and one-third of overall spending (Schwartz and Woloshin 2019). Another trend has been the increase in digital advertising within the industry: eMarketer indicated that US healthcare and pharmaceutical advertisers increased their digital ad spending by 20.1% to $3.62 Billion in 2019 (Benes 2019).

Additionally, the nature of DTC advertising has also changed, shifting from demographic-based targeting and endemic websites to increasingly focusing on spending money wisely and ensuring they are reaching audiences with specific health histories. To that end, media vehicles like programmatic digital advertising, and addressable television enable greater precision than ever before. In short, the pharmaceutical industry, like packaged goods or financial services industry before it, has now adopted data-driven *targeting* methodologies.

These are the most important success criteria in this new age of targeting:

- *Reach*: Deploying advertising to a significant percentage of the relevant patient population of interest. For a marketer of a prostate cancer medication, the wish is serve ads to as many prostate cancer patients as possible.
- *Precision*: Serving ads to those with a combination of specific health characteristics. In the prostate cancer example, precision can mean reaching patients diagnosed with metastatic castration-resistant prostate cancer (mCRPC) who also take zoledronic acid. This focused patient profile

allows media to reach an audience that is eligible for the advertised brand and more likely to be ready for this treatment option.

- *Privacy*: Not specifically targeting consumers by utilizing personally identifiable information such as name, address, health conditions, or history.
- *Cost efficiency*: Minimizing wasted media spending on unqualified consumers while also minimizing the cost per qualified audience reached.

Of the different targeting criteria listed above, there is a fundamental tradeoff between *precision and privacy*. The more targeting aims to precisely reach consumers with certain conditions, the higher the risk of identifying individuals. This is especially true for rare conditions, which are increasingly the domain of new pharmaceutical products.

Different targeting mechanisms have aimed to address the precision vs. privacy tradeoff in distinct ways. Table 6.3 describes three leading healthcare targeting methods.

- *Endemic publishers*: Placing ads on condition pages and treatment information on health portal websites where consumers seek information. This approach avoids targeting privacy issues in that the consumer voluntarily visits these pages and views the ads searching for information. They tend to have low reach, but very high precision, since the audience is self-selecting as having a diagnosis or treating with drugs in the category. Because of the high precision, such websites tend to charge a high cost.
- *Predictive models*: Privacy in targeting is accomplished by using predictive models whose inputs are not health related. The approach is much like credit-scoring in banking: publicly available data like demographics, socio-economics, and financial transactions are inputs into a machine-learning model that predicts likelihood of having a disease or taking a medication.

TABLE 6.3 Comparison of Three Leading Healthcare Media Targeting Methods

Targeting Method	Description	Privacy Method	Reach	Precision	Cost ($CPM)
Endemic publishers	Place ads on health condition websites.	Voluntary consumer website visits	Low	Very high	High
Predictive models	Serve ads to high-scoring consumers of a predictive model.	Inputs are publicly available demographic and socioeconomic variables	Medium	Medium to high	Medium
Hyperlocal geographies	Serve ads to hyperlocal geographies having definitive claims-based evidence of target patients	Target a hyperlocal geography rather than individuals, by leveraging multi-year datasets	Medium	Medium to high	Medium

The likelihood score is used to rank consumers (and their digital devices) for targeting. Reach can be high, depending on the score threshold utilized. Cost is typically lower than endemic ad placement. Precision is typically medium because non-health variables may not be sufficient predictors of health behaviors; on occasion, these models can have high precision, but must be monitored.

- *Hyperlocal areas*: This method utilizes a comprehensive geographic and multi-year data asset of validated real-world medical and prescription claims data to find hyperlocal areas with patients meeting the desired healthcare profile over a multi-year time period. Privacy is met via the generalized time and geographic dimensions. Precision is medium to high, and is particularly valuable in rare diseases. Reach is mid-level. Cost is lower compared to healthcare endemic sites.

In my experience analyzing data from multiple digital healthcare media campaign I have seen both predictive models and hyperlocal geography targeting provide nearly comparable targeting precision at a significantly higher efficiency than endemic publishers. Brand marketers, however, need to have some presence on the endemic websites to be there for the "lower funnel" consumers who are actively seeking information. They will not leave this valuable real estate to competitive brands.

6.5 Conclusions

In this chapter, we have reviewed the different components of promotional targeting and the role of big data analytics in driving promotion to desirable segments. Alternative targeting methods have different profiles on success criteria such as reach, precision, and cost efficiency.

This chapter and the prior one have revealed that segmentation and targeting are closely linked concepts; the targeted set of consumers can be considered a defacto segment. Alternatively, a segment that has desirable purchase behaviors historically can be used for targeting.

Targeting in a broader sense also includes delivering the right message at the right time for the desirable audience. Therefore, it is important to understand and analyze the priority touchpoints of your priority segments, and to employ predictive models for understanding what messaging has previously driven a response.

6.6 Exercises

1. A field sales representative has 400 clients or prospects in her territory. She can visit with up to ten clients per day, and works 48 weeks Monday through Friday during the year. The representative has to use headquarters analytics output to devise a targeting approach.

a) If she wanted her target list to allow for visiting each targeted customer every week, how many clients could she afford to target? What percentage is that of the territory?

b) She reviews the analytics and decides that 150 clients are worth visiting during the year.

Complete the table below with one or more scenarios to allow her to reach those clients:

Segment	Visit Frequency	Count
Gold	Once per week	
Silver	Once per 2 weeks	
Bronze	Once per 4 weeks	
Total		150

2. Digital display advertising is bought using a rate of *cost per thousand impressions*, or CPM. Say purchasing display ads with a programmatic vendor has a CPM of $12 and on an endemic website the CPM is $30.

a) If a client has a budget of $1.8 million to spend on a digital media campaign, how many impressions could be served if only on endemic websites? If only on programmatic placements?

b) Say the audience quality of endemic websites is 6%, and the quality for the programmatic channel is 4%. Presume each consumer gets five impressions on average. For the same $1.8 million budget, how many qualified diagnosed patients would be reached with only the endemic publisher? With only the programmatic publisher?

c) With a 50/50 spend split between endemic and programmatic, and the same $1.8 million budget, how many qualified patients will be reached in total?

3. Say you are an online retailer, and have done a segmentation exercise of your transactional customer database. Of the ten segments, one has the behavior of initially high purchasers that subsequently decrease spending on your brand.

a) Would you make this segment a target?

b) If so, when would you promote to them, in what channel, and what message would you provide?

Note

1 This section has been adapted from an abstract and presentation at the Pharmaceutical Management Science Association while the author was employed at Medicx Health (Evans and Haimowitz 2021).

7
CAMPAIGN MEASUREMENT WITH LEARNING OBJECTIVES

Companies have been investing significantly in marketing measurement. According to the pre-pandemic 2019 CMO Survey (Moorman 2019) corporate marketers invested 6% to 8% of their marketing budget on marketing analytics and planned to spend 10%–13% over the following 3 years. For brands spending tens of millions of dollars on promotion (media, sales calls, social, direct marketing), that planned annual measurement investment promised to be in the millions.

There are three primary objectives of measuring a promotional campaign:

1. Determine the financial impact for the company.
2. Learn about your audience's background and how they responded.
3. Identify key performance drivers for future optimization.

On this latter point, note that optimization is multi-dimensional, covering spend, channel, frequency, creative, and message.

We will cover how to achieve each of these three measurement objectives in depth over the course of this chapter. First, we will introduce two core concepts: *measurement planning* for campaigns, and the necessary *data acquisition and integration*.

7.1 Start with a Measurement Plan

Even before you launch your campaign, it pays to plan which business questions you are looking to answer and what metrics will help answer those questions. The timing is early to gain alignment and plan on sourcing the right data.

DOI: 10.4324/9780429300363-9

TABLE 7.1 Example Measurement Plan for a Promotional Campaign

Measurement Objectives	Specific Questions	Metrics and Data Required	Business Decisions
Reaching a Quality Audience	• Am I reaching the right demographic? • Is my audience eligible for my product or service? • How much waste is in my reach?		
Impacting the Customer Journey	• Is audience consuming content on our owned properties? • Are they moving down the customer journey? • How many new customer conversions? • Are customers increasingly loyal?		
Return on Investment	• What is financial impact on incremental revenue? • How does incremental revenue compare to spend? • Which channels are driving return?		
Promotional Optimization	• How efficient is my outreach to prospects? • How can I reallocate my spending and frequency across channels to improve return? • What messages can be optimized?		

Furthermore, the types of data and analytic techniques you use to measure will depend in part on these business objectives.

This is a discipline I have recommended before for relationship marketing programs (Haimowitz 2011). Really though, measurement planning is applicable for any promotional campaign, whether consumer or professional, and whether driven by paid media, field forces, public relations, or any combination thereof. See Table 7.1 for an outline of a measurement plan that is general enough for measuring a promotional campaign, whether it is aimed at consumers or professionals.

7.1.1 Components of the Measurement Plan

The measurement plan is organized by category of objectives, and within each objective are specific questions that you'd wish to answer regarding your promotional campaign. In the table, these are listed in the two left columns.

Consider for example a particular advertising initiative: a direct-to-consumer media campaign for a health-related, demographic specific branded product. Given this, let's step through the objectives and questions suggested in the table:

• Reaching a Quality Audience: The questions relate to whether those exposed to the promotion are in the right demographic, and if they are qualified or eligible for the promoted product or service. In the healthcare example, this can mean understanding what percentage of those reached by the campaign are diagnosed with the disease that the product treats (Haimowitz and Kemper 2018; Miller 2021).

- Impacting the Customer Journey: These questions relate to how those receiving the promotion or advertisement change their behavior, specifically as to whether they are increasing engagement with the advertiser's assets and moving further along the purchase path. In the pharmaceutical example, measurement could test if those exposed to the advertising are visiting a specialist, engaging with the ad, or ultimately receiving the product.
- Return on Investment: This objective assesses the incremental revenue attributed to this campaign, and compares to investment, with hopes of isolating specific channels that are most impactful. In the healthcare example, incremental patients on brand can be quantified and extrapolated as added revenue, and compared to costs of media, creative development, and patient support. The new patients can be analyzed based on which channels they were exposed to: digital display vs. paid search vs. television vs. print, etc.
- Promotion Optimization: These questions aim to uncover the factors that contribute to the success or failure of the campaign, and the specific changes that can be made to improve return. In the medical example, this might relate to shifting advertising spend among different media publishers. Another option could be shifting the messaging of the campaign to increasingly emphasize services associated with the product.

7.1.2 Measurement Planning Additional Details

Associated with each set of objectives and questions are more tactical details. One has to identify *specific metrics* to evaluate for answering those questions, and what data are required to calculate those metrics.

Let's consider the assessment of audience qualification for a healthcare advertisement. This can be expressed as a percentage of those exposed who have evidence of a diagnosis. The data required could vary; examples are:

- a survey question to consumers who recall the ad and
- actual medical claims associated with patients known to have received an impression.

Short descriptions of metrics and data sources may be sufficient for a summarized measurement plan table. However, building an operational measurement system requires further details that may span many pages, including coding schemes, vendor partners, and data file transfer protocols. Dedicated staff is required to make sure accurate measurement is set up and delivers consistent, quality results.

7.1.3 Consequences of Measurement on Business Action

To make your measurement results impact business decisions, the joint analytics and business team should explicitly plan in advance what actions will be taken when particular metrics achieve particular thresholds. Here are two hypothetical examples:

- If a media source (medical publisher, search keyword) has a cost-per-qualified audience of greater than $100 and the campaign has run for 2 months or more, then stop funding that media source, and shift the remaining dollars to the most efficient media source as possible.
- If the return on investment is projected as negative after 3 months in market, cancel the campaign.

These rules demonstrate that metrics are more impactful if they are continually monitored over time during a campaign, in order to make optimization midstream. Otherwise, metrics are merely lessons learned for future campaigns. If such mid-course corrections are desirable, then data collection must be built with an appropriate frequency and a minimal time lag.

7.1.4 Key Performance Indicators

Of the many marketing campaign metrics to evaluate, several are designated as *key performance indicators*. Frankly, I have found this a subjective and ambiguous designation that can vary across industries and brands. Here are some criteria for choosing which few metrics should be included as a KPI:

- Provide an aggregated status of campaign success
- Can be quickly and dynamically updated
- Easy to understand by senior management

Let's return to our example of a consumer healthcare media campaign. Here are some proposed KPIs that meet the above criteria:

- Cumulative diagnosed patients reached;
- Cost per qualified patient reached
- Cumulative new patient support enrollees

By contrast, here are two examples of inferior KPIs: total ad exposures served and number of sales calls made. These are measures of media or promotional activity, without necessarily indicating a potential business impact.

7.2 Data Integration for Campaign Measurement

Measuring a media or promotional campaign is undoubtedly a big data analytics activity. Measurement requires integrating distinct databases that link promotional exposure to brand and category performance, followed by multivariate analyses to assess campaign lift.

As shown in Figure 7.1, at minimum three types of information assets must be combined:

1. Promotional exposure: quantifying the levels of audience exposure for each promotional channel over time. Let's consider display (banner) advertising aimed at consumers as an example. Data can be provided multiple ways:
   - Impression counts by time period (say daily, weekly, or monthly) for each digital channel: all programmatic segments, endemic publishers, lifestyle publishers, etc.
   - Cost information of these media impressions: dollars spent per each of the media channels in each time period. These costs can be supplementary or a replacement for the impression data.
   - Detailed individual-level exposure data: For each person reached, accounting for a number of ad exposures across each channel. These can be transactional per impression, or summarized by channel and day.
2. Audience attributes: these provide extra descriptive profiling characteristics for additional insights into campaign results, or serve as sub-dimensions for separate analyses. Sticking with the consumer display campaign example, such attributes might include:
   - Demographics, including geography, age, gender, ethnicity, or economic status.
   - Lifestyles, such as hobbies, or health habits like diet and exercise levels.
   - Media habits, including preferred communication channels, and types of devices used for consuming content. As one example, in what ratio are the audiences consuming television with cable TV, satellite packages, or mobile streaming devices?

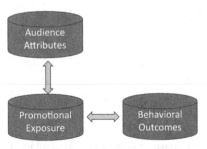

FIGURE 7.1 Integrated Data Sets Required for Promotional Campaign Analytics

Where do these attributes come from? Often they are based on survey-based data where a sample respondents' answers are modeled or projected to various levels of geography, for use in matching to a promotional campaign.

3. Purchase-based outcomes data. Ultimately, to measure sales or marketing campaign effectiveness, sales-related outcome measures are needed. Thus, the analysis requires purchase-based activity in a sequential time period that can be potentially attributed to the promotion. In a digital media campaign for E-commerce, the online product sales for advertised brands are required.

The level of granularity of these data elements will determine how detailed your analysis can be and what results you can attain in your measurement plan. More on this is in the next section.

7.3 Analytic Methods for Promotional Campaign Evaluation

Let's get specific about the methods of analyzing multi-channel campaign re-sults. In my experience working across industries, our teams have fielded three predominant methodologies for measuring campaign impact: marketing mix, holdout samples, and multi-touch attribution. We will provide an overview of each of these methods.

7.3.1 Marketing Mix Analysis

Marketing mix is an established decades-old approach, with foundations i time-series statistical analysis. Historical aggregated exposures (or spend) by channel are inputs, and sales by time period are the output. Mathematically, a typical marketing mix equation is:

$$\left[S_t = b_0 + \sum_{(i=1)}^{n} b_i * x_{(t, i)} \right]$$

where S_t represents the sales at time t, and the X_i denotes the n marketing channel variables that drive sales. The estimated coefficients b_i in this model can be used to provide the relative importance of each channel.

A common granularity of inputs is 2 years of weekly national exposure data across channels combined with 2 years of sales. A more detailed analysis within the US is to provide similar inputs at the designated market area (DMA) level, representing over 200 geographic metro areas, especially when the marketing plans show significant geographic variation.

A good foundation of marketing mix analysis and its applicability to analyze sales in the face of brand switching and competition is (Carpenter and Leh-mann 1985). There have been a range of extensions and nuances for specific channel analyses. Blankfein et al. (2017) in a presentation at the Advertising Research Foundation conference, develop models contrasting the relative contributions of television, digital and social media. Weiner et al. (2010) have developed mix models for isolating the effects of public relations activity on sales. Other articles have noted special treatment required for word of mouth (Fay and Larkin 2017) and cross-channel (Fulgoni and Lipsman 2017; Snyder and Garcia-Garcia 2016).

One valuable output of marketing mix is that outputs can be used to generate a waterfall chart that quantifies the contribution to sales. As shown in Figure 7.2, say the most recent time period has sales of $110 million dollars. The marketing mix can break down that $100 million of this is *base sales,* essentially a carryover from prior time periods, but not due to any promotional effects. The different bars in the chart demonstrate the TV advertising contributed $3.8 million in incremental revenue, display advertising $3.7 million, and so on with other positive media factors. The primary negative factor was pricing increases, which led to a $2.8 million decrease in sales.

Marketing mix solutions also lend themselves to simulations and sensitivity analyses, where hypothetical adjustments can be made to channel media spend, with a calculation of the resulting sales lift.

There are a series of pre-modeling data engineering steps required for implementing marketing mix analyses. One is cleansing, and mapping all input media sources into a standardized format resulting in similar scales of magnitude. Another often-applied technique is *adstocking,* which extends the impact of media investment at time t to have partial media impact at future time periods, usually modeled as a decreasing exponential function.

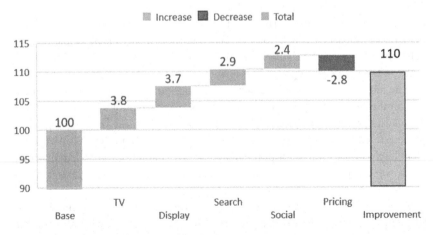

FIGURE 7.2 Marketing Mix "Waterfall" Decomposition of Channel Impact on Sales

Coming back to our measurement plan, a marketing mix solution can measure the impact of a campaign in terms of incremental sales and ROI, and it can also enable optimization, usually at the macro channel level. However, the solution is not designed to assess audience quality of the reached audience, or to measure impact on customers along their journey.

7.3.2 Lift Over Holdout Sample

If your objective is primarily to assess the sales lift and the return on investment from your campaign, then the most straightforward analysis technique is to have a stratified, random holdout sample. One selects a random subset of prospects that would be eligible for promotion, often 5% or 10% of the available prospects. Do not send a promotion to that group. Track the reached audience to the holdout sample for future behavior and incremental revenue. Comparing the difference in the incremental sales determines the impact of the promotion, and that impact can then be extrapolated to the total market to get an overall impact lift.

One non-obvious question is how to choose the holdout sample. Usually, this is through a random selection of some kind. A programming language as basic as SQL can be used to select every Nth record from a database. Another option: if each member of your population has a numerical account number that is generated incrementally, then choose based on digits, such as:

- Take all account numbers ending in "3" to choose a random 10% as a holdout
- Take all accounts ending in "3X" where X is between 1 and 5 inclusive to choose a random 5% holdout.

Although the holdout sample approach is fairly straightforward, it is not universally employed. This is primarily because many marketing directors intent on driving top-line revenue do not want to relinquish any promotional targets. Selecting a 10% holdout sample from 1 million eligible prospects means that 100,000 are not receiving a promotion.

The alternative to a holdout sample is to use "natural experiments," which rely on the unexposed population to form the selection pool of a control group. Take a field force promotion to business accounts. Presume the sales representatives are expected to record every visit to a prospect, and that information is completely captured in a corporate database. By matching the called-on prospects over a time period to the full prospect database, one can select as controls the prospects who were not promoted.

Another example is consumer media measurement, because in a media campaign not every person or every household will be reached. If you are gathering exposure data with a high capture rate, then you can infer that the individuals missing from your data sample were not reached. Those non-reached consumers can form the basis of a control group for comparison.

7.3.3 Design of Experiments

A design of experiments for a promotional campaign aims to answer the question: which of a set of controllable factors is most driving impact, such as incremental sales, or response rate? The methodology essentially is based on these three steps:

1. Deploy in market alternative combinations of values of the various factors to distinct, yet similar sets of the eligible population.
2. Collect results on the key response variable for each fielded combination
3. Analyze which levels on each factor perform best, and which factors most impact the outcome. Statistical significance of the factor impacts is often evaluated with analysis of variance (ANOVA).

Additional methodological details can be found in Dean and Voss (1998).

The most basic design of experiments is an A/B Test, where two alternatives to a single dimension are considered. An example would be two alternative creative executions of an email, and possible outcomes can be open rates, click-through rates, or purchase conversion.

Note that in Step 1 above, usually one cannot realistically field campaign branches on all combinations. Such an execution is called a *full factorial*, and the alternatives grow exponentially. For example, if there are N factors each with three levels, there are 3^N combinations, which means 81 branches for four factors and 243 for five factors. To save on this complexity, a *fractional factorial* set of combinations can be executed that chooses a subset of the alternatives that are sufficient for outcome analysis. Database marketing-specific software packages can generate such combinations.

In my time working for direct marketing agencies, I have designed and implemented a series of multi-factor design of experiment campaigns on a large scale, either via direct mail or email. Variables tested included:

- Personalized message (name, behavioral segment) vs. general message
- Creative execution options
- Financial offer variations (such as a coupon or a price)

In these cases, dozens of combinations were tried according to a fractional factorial specification, and highest performing levels were determined and analyzed for significance.

7.3.4 Multi-Touch Attribution

If your firm has a data-rich environment consisting of longitudinal customer-level transaction data, then you may be able to employ multi-touch attribution, which lets you gain in-depth insights as to how your campaign is affecting the behavior of your reached audience.

Multi-touch attribution pulls together many of the concepts discussed earlier in this chapter. Coming back to Figure 7.1, the level of matching between promotional exposure and behavioral outcomes is at the individual level. Ideally, the behaviors consist of years of detailed transactions prior to the campaign, and continuing during and after the consumers first see your promotion. If so, that enables customer-level metrics to answer the questions on audience quality and customer journey, within the measurement plan of Table 7.1.

To see how this comes together, consider the individual customer timeline illustrated in Figure 7.3. Several key points and time windows are aligned on a timeline spanning months to years.

The central data point, in bold, is the date this prospect is first exposed to the promotional campaign; call that date $D0$. An audience quality look-back time window of T days is used to check whether this prospect is qualified. There may be many definitions of a qualified audience, but here we will use a definition of a purchase of a competitive product. For this particular prospect, there is a behavior record of the competitive purchase 75 days before exposure to the ad, and 75 days is less than the time window T, which is say 90 days. Thus, we would say this reached prospect was qualified.

Looking to the right of this data point is a second-time window, for *conversion attribution*. This is a time range, in days to months, for evaluating whether or not the exposed prospect has changed their behavior as a consequence, such as purchasing the advertised product. In Figure 7.3, the prospect purchases the advertised brand 26 days after first seeing the ad. Now say the attribution time window is 60 days; since 26 days is within the attribution time window, that patient is said to be a conversion based on the campaign.

The results illustrated here for one prospect are in practice aggregated across the entire exposed audience, and resulting metrics such as *audience quality rate* and *conversion rate* are computed and can feed into the measurement plan for

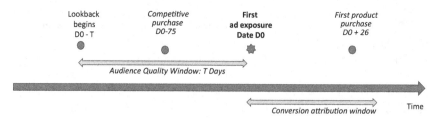

FIGURE 7.3 Illustrative Timeline for Audience Quality and Conversion

campaign evaluation. Those rates, in turn, can be combined with total audience reach volumes to project totals for qualified audience and new conversions.

Note that in some promotional channels and some industries, the individual matching referenced here may be highly regulated and partially incomplete. In our later chapter on data privacy, we go into more detail on how these constraints are currently navigated and plan to face additional restrictions.

Another important point is worth noting: in the above reasoning, as results are aggregated, there is an assumption that your transactional behavioral data is complete and accurately reflects a prospect's behavior. This assumption may not always hold, and so it is important that you perform the calculations of qualified audience percentage and conversion purchase percentage on *eligible* populations where there is reasonable assurance of continuity of behavior captured. A strong analytics group should build in eligibility checks within their measurement process.

Finally, these treatments presented here are shown for a monolithic campaign and an overall evaluation. In reality, promotional campaigns consist of multiple media sources, which may or may not overlap in terms of the prospects reached. One exercise at end of this chapter explores how to determine separate audience quality calculations. For conversions to the advertised brand, overlaps need to be apportioned based on heuristics or algorithms. Early approaches to apportioning "credit" for new customer conversions were based on recency of exposure before the purchase, or frequency of exposure. A more recent method gaining popularity, also found in Python and R coding libraries, is the *Shapley algorithm*; details of this approach can be found in Zhao et al. (2018).

7.3.5 Return on Investment

Many of the campaign measurement techniques described in this section can enable a return on investment (ROI) calculation. At its most fundamental, ROI can be calculated thusly:

$$\text{ROI of campaign} = \frac{\text{incremental revenue attributed to campaign} - \text{total campaign costs}}{(\text{total campaign costs})}$$

With this formulation, in a "break-even" scenario where incremental revenue equals total campaign costs, the ROI value is zero. Some companies may choose to omit the subtraction in the numerator, in which case a break-even ROI value is one.

The attribution of incremental revenue to a campaign depends on its objectives:

- If the goal is purely to add new customers, then determine the incremental number of new customers, and estimate a lifetime value per new customer.

- Determining a "new customer" requires business rules that leverage a customer's transactional history. How long back in time do you look before ad exposure for the absence of that product? How long forward in time do you allow post-ad exposure for the product conversion to be attributed to the promotion? What impression frequency do you base these time windows on?
- If the goal is to increase revenue from existing customers, then an incremental spend amount over a matched control group or a baseline should be incorporated. Again, a time window of looking forward post-promotion is required.
- There may also be campaign objectives related to saving money, such as getting customers to register for online statements that will reduce production and postal delivery fees. These expense savings can be translated into revenue as well.
- One final thought on revenue: companies may choose whether to use gross revenue or net. I have seen gross revenue used more often, so that future operational efficiencies do not necessarily affect campaign ROI.

Now, let's turn out attention to costs. If the only cost being considered is the advertising expenditures, then the ROI calculation is often called ROAS, or *return on ad spend*. However, usually there are other costs related to a sales or marketing campaign, including the following:

- Creative development and production
- Postage and other delivery fees, if applicable
- Agency and vendor account management fees

These costs and others can be combined with the sum of advertising-related costs to have a more realistic ROI calculation.

7.4 Learning about Your Campaign's Audience and Response

The process of campaign measurement is an excellent opportunity to go beyond strictly numerical assessment and really answer questions about your reached audience, whether they are established customers, new prospects, or a mix. When you run a marketing promotion, ask your organization: how much are you learning from your campaign evaluation?

7.4.1 Simple Yet Probing Questions

Especially within a business environment, where communication clarity is paramount, I've found it helpful to pose the learning opportunities in terms of straightforward questions[1]:

- Who is the campaign reaching?

Is your campaign reaching intended targets that you may have conceptualized based on prior small-scale market research studies and quantitative segmentation analyses? These insights can be evaluated using retrospective transaction analysis as exemplified in Figure 7.3. If you can further match that behavioral data with demographics and socioeconomics data as Figure 7.1 suggests, then the audience quality insights will be even deeper. Another way to get at these results is through advertising awareness market research studies, but there you risk projecting insights from a small sample.

- What actions is your reached audience taking?

Are those exposed to your ads subsequently responding as you have designed? Again, as shown in Figure 7.3, transactions will reveal if individuals are taking offline behaviors. One example relevant to pharmaceutical advertising: a patient post-exposure visiting a physician specialist, getting a laboratory test, receiving a new diagnosis, and ultimately, receiving a prescription for the advertised brand.

- Why are they responding?

This can be determined through sub-analysis by population cohorts divided by actionable dimensions. For example, are certain demographic or attitudinal traits associated with higher response rates? Does your media plan have the right impression frequency to drive desired behavior change? Could your product pricing be mismatched with the economic realities of whom you are messaging? Having such insights can help you adapt your targeting or messaging approach mid-stream.

7.4.2 A Brief Case Study

Consider a hypothetical (but realistic) pharmaceutical digital media campaign for a condition prevalent in an older, female population. To answer why the audience may or may not be responding, a set of consumer attribute information was matched to three populations: a national baseline, the full reached audience, and those reached who were verified to have a prior diagnosis of the targeted condition. The resulting average scores are shown in Figure 7.4.

As shown in the figure, the reached and diagnosed audience (bar at right) is less likely to participate in yoga compared to the national baseline or compared to all reached consumers. However, the reached diagnosed audience is highly rated as conscientious information seekers, meaning they would benefit from additional patient education materials. These are two examples of how in-depth data integration can stimulate a re-thinking of creative imagery and messaging for the next campaign wave.

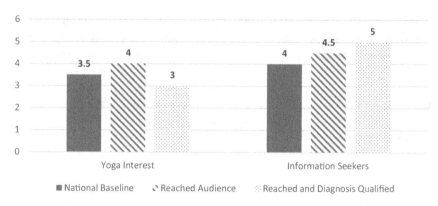

FIGURE 7.4 Illustrative Differences in Attributes in Reached Audience vs. Baseline

This example is really just scratching the surface of potential insights that one can uncover, based on the data assets available. Further in-depth treatment of these learning criteria for campaign measurement, including a detailed analysis of a similar digital media study, can be found in a recent *PM360* healthcare trade journal issue (Haimowitz 2021).

7.5 Ongoing Performance Monitoring and Optimization

In sales or marketing campaigns, one should be continually monitoring results and be prepared to make intermediate course corrections. These changes can bring higher net revenue impact and improve cost efficiency. This monitoring can occur on a daily, weekly, or monthly basis depending on the decision-making cycle of your company, and the refresh rate of your data inputs and performance metric calculations.

Examples of monitoring that can yield campaign optimizations are as follows:

- Tracking which media channels are most cost effectively driving new customers
- Seeing which audience segments are most responsive, and adjusting promotional weight accordingly
- Correlating ad frequency with post-exposure action rates
- Testing responses of alternative creative or messages

Let's now come back to the customer journey objective from measurement planning that we described at the beginning of this chapter. If you define behavioral segments based on the customer journey, and you label your prospect database by segment, then you can track over time how prospects move from one segment to another. I have implemented this approach with sales management in B-to-B settings, and it proved effective for clarity and motivational effect.

7.6 Conclusions

Integrated data and analytics can enable a continuous campaign evaluation and learning process that runs in an ongoing business cycle. As we will discuss in a later chapter, this process is often termed *closed-loop marketing*, meaning that outcomes from each wave of promotion contribute to improvements in future waves. With the proper planning, measurement, and tracking, a company can continually optimize return and cost efficiencies, and gain further insights at each turn.

The campaign measurement approaches within this chapter provide a foundational framework that can be extended and automated with machine learning across campaigns and channels. If you have run tens, or hundreds of campaigns within the same product category, each across different media channels, then you are primed to have a campaign-level data set for meta-analysis and learning. Later in this book, we address similar issues in a chapter on Knowledge Management.

7.7 Exercises

1. Consider a marketing campaign that you are involved in at your company, or otherwise that you have been exposed to as a consumer.
   a) Develop a measurement plan for that campaign based on the outline in Table 7.1. Determine what relevant business questions you wish to answer, and identify the associated metrics and data to help answer those questions.
   b) What business decisions would you make if certain values were above or below expectations?
2. Your company is executing an email campaign to your customer database of 1 million members. Your head of marketing would like to test three different creative executions and two different offers.
   a) Given the options outlined in this chapter, what analysis design would you select?
   b) How many distinct campaign executions would you field in-market?
   c) How would you divide the 1 million customers accordingly?

3. By employing multi-touch attribution in a consumer digital media campaign, you are able to assemble the following information half-way through the project:

Media Source	Consumers Reached	Qualified Consumers	Cost for Media	Incremental New Customers
Programmatic segment	150,000	31,600	$2,800	350
Lifestyle demographic website	320,000	54,000	$6,500	480
Domain-specific endemic website	80,000	28,500	$3,200	360

Given these data, please answer the following:

a) Which of the media sources has the highest audience quality rate?
b) Which has the most efficient cost per qualified audience?
c) Assuming there is no overlap in reach, which is the most cost-efficient at generating new customers?
d) Again assuming no reach overlap, if the lifetime value of a new customer is $1,100; what is the return on ad spend for the overall campaign?
e) Would you make any shifts of media spend to optimize for the second half of the campaign? Why or why not?

Note

1 This framework was utilized during my tenure at Medicx Health, for example.

8

STRATEGIC TEXT MINING

In the past 10 years, there has been a dramatic increase in collection, processing, and analytics of unstructured text data, for the purpose of commercial applications: sales, marketing, and corporate communications.

"Unstructured" data means it cannot be placed into a traditional tabular structure befitting a relational database. Free text, speech wave files, and images are common forms of unstructured data. In order to extract insightful analyses, some structure must be imposed.

Before discussing the analytics methodology for text mining, let's first discuss some of the business applications.

8.1 Corporate Strategy Opportunities for Big Data

Chief Communications and Chief Marketing Officers, and Heads of Market Analytics groups are all responsible for strategic analysis in their companies. Toward that end, they need to follow the conversations taking place among their stakeholders, many of which are listed in Figure 8.1.

A stakeholder is a group of people that have an interest in the actions and reputation of a company. The stakeholders listed in the figure include:

- Customers and prospective customers, who are describing their needs in the category and their perceptions of the different products available in the market
- Investors and financial analysts that are evaluating the policies and financial outlook of the company to determine whether to create or maintain a position

DOI: 10.4324/9780429300363-10

FIGURE 8.1 Stakeholders Writing Text-Based Reviews Affecting Corporate Strategy

- Academics and other thought leaders who are evaluating a company based on their record of innovation and research and development pipeline
- Employees and job candidates who are evaluating their experience or their prospects of working at the firm

Indeed, the stakeholders help form the reputation of that company, through their perceptions and their communications about that firm. Each of these is communicated through text sources of various types.

Below we itemize a series of related business applications that utilize unstructured text mining. Then we go into technical details of analytic methodology.

8.2 Business Applications Leveraging Text Mining

Below are a range of applied business challenges that especially rely on text-based data:

- Brand sentiment analysis: Understanding what the opinion is of brand users or company followers, expressed on a scale of −1 (negative), 0 (neutral), or 1 (positive). The analysis is often done on streams of social media posts, like Twitter tweets. Aggregated over a set of posts, the result ranges from −1 to +1 and can be considered a "net sentiment" score. The net sentiment score can be monitored over time, as shown in Figure 8.2, which compares sentiment for two companies on a weekly basis. In the figure, Company A has shown a recent decrease in sentiment, and company B has been rising weekly from net negative sentiment to net positive. Note that sentiment can be at the overall company level, for a specific brand, topic, or policy.
- Category landscape: Providing an overview of the major topics being discussed or written about within a particular category. Especially helpful for quickly understanding an industry by digesting publications and news articles. Usually, results are visualized as a cluster analysis through similarity measures between articles.
- Competitive intelligence: Knowing the product pipelines, positioning, and latest commercial activities of competitive companies and their

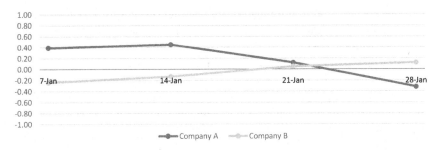

FIGURE 8.2 Tracking Sentiment Analysis Weekly for Two Companies

products. These can be discerned from academic conference reports, press releases, and newswires. Indeed, a competitive intelligence analysis can be a by-product of a category landscape, mentioned above.

- Needs of stakeholders: Identifying the unmet needs of customers, prospects, academics, and other industry professionals, based on industry blogs and reviews. The unmet needs may be valuable in identifying ideas for new product development. To discern these needs, text-mining searches for domain-specific product and action phrases coupled with intention-based expressions or sentiment indicators.
- Issue monitoring: Keeping track of levels of mentions of controversial topics that could affect the company's reputation. One example is a quick-service restaurant that is linked to animal cruelty practices of its suppliers. Upticks in this chatter need to be detected quickly in order to plan a public response.
- Reputation analysis: Evaluating the perception of one's company vs. competitors along the most important purchasing decision factors. One growing example is a company's reputation with respect to environmental, social, and governance (ESG) issues such as sustainability. Companies that pollute or manufacture products contributing to waste (like single use plastics) can suffer in reputation and lose potential investors. The prominence of ESG as an investor consideration has increased dramatically as described in Harvard Business Review (2011), Howard-Grenville (2021), Review (2011) and Rahman et al. (2017).

8.3 Sources of Unstructured Text Data

Given the need to evaluate the comments and perceptions of stakeholders, what are the data sources to pursue that have these comments?

Social Media consists of short digital posts within connected groups:

- General social media and groups: Contains peer-to-peer comments, reviews, and sentiments related to products from users and prospects.

- Specialized communities: These are websites, groups, or chatrooms dedicated to a particular topic, and often result in more in-depth comments. One example are travel review sites and communities, that can go into significant detail on accomodations, transportation, attractions, and service.

Owned Media are properties that a brand creates and controls content of. As such, owned media can include strategic information for reputation or competitive analyses, including the following:

- Press Releases often reveal new product launches, executive appointments, or new corporate initiatives.
- Corporate Earnings Reports, for publicly traded companies, provide financial information and trends, often at the country and product line level.

Earned Media are articles written about a company by either news outlets or other independent reporters from well-followed sources, such as:

- Blogs are written by respected leaders in an industry and may include opinions or assessments of companies, their strategies, and leading brands.
- News coverage are articles in print, TV or online networks or news sources, that cover events related to a company or its causes.
- Industry journals and conference proceedings provide foundations within an industry and corporate capability assessments.
- Rating organizations (example: Gartner, Consumer Reports, Motor Trend) provide articles with reputable company and product assessments.

Paid media is not always text based, often consisting of video or imagery. Examples are banners, online videos, print ads, and search responses. However, paid advertising can be a valid source for branded product attributes, and core messaging that companies use to differentiate vs. competitors.

8.4 Building Blocks of Text Mining

What are the modules required to build a system that mines text to gather the marketplace intelligence? We list core components and briefly describe their functionality here. For a more detailed treatment, we recommend an in-depth book on text mining such as Anandarajan et al. (2019) or Bengfort et al. (2018).

- *Syntax and semantics modules*: These are required for processing raw text files or posts, separating these into sentences, and extracting meaningful units like subjects, actions, and objects acted upon or referred to. Pronouns and ellipsis are identified and resolved to specific noun phrases.

- *Stakeholder Identification:* How do you determine whether text messages come from a particular stakeholder, whether customers, reviewers, employees, or academic thought leaders? There are three primary methods:
  - *Specialized data sources:* Some text corpuses are defined by a stakeholder. Glassdoor includes a section on employee reviews; Yelp is specific to reviews for products and services. Conference proceedings or related blogs are the voice of academics or industry researchers.
  - *Self-identification:* in the message itself an author may describe their relationship: "I am a <Brand X> customer and have the following opinion."
  - *Public profiles:* within a (public) profile of an account generating the text source, as in a social media account that describes a Mother of two from New Jersey.
- *Domain Specific Taxonomies:* To process text within a specific industry such as medicine, retail, or high technology, particular dictionaries of critical words must be created, and taxonomies established to help group subject matter.
  - An example of this related to analysis of hypertension within social media streams was articulated in Haimowitz and Obata (2009). The objective of that research was to classify and separate out conversations related to symptoms, treatments, and other lifestyle adjustments.

Communications analytics vendors and public relations agencies conduct corporate reputation analyses relying on industry-specific taxonomies consisting of dozens to hundreds of terms. A partial outline is illustrated in Figure 8.3.

Due to space limitations, the figure shows a partial taxonomy for strategic text analyses of a packaged goods corporation for competitive intelligence or reputation scorecards. As shown in the figure, dialogue specific to analyzing a company can fall into multiple *dimensions*: listed here are financial news about the company's performance and investments, product-related news, and policies related to ESG (environmental, social, and governance). Other dimensions could be employee relations and innovation.

The next deeper level are *topics*; within ESG this can include waste, pollution, carbon footprint, and ethics. Below topics are *tactics*, which refer to specific actions the company has taken or plans to. Pictured below carbon footprint is

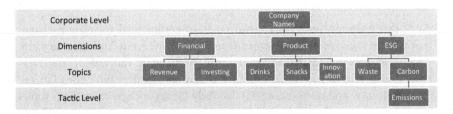

FIGURE 8.3   Partial Industry Specific Taxonomy for Corporate Strategic Analyses

a tactic of emissions. There are multiple tactics per topic, not pictured in the figure due to space considerations.

How is this taxonomy applied? Say the news articles analyzed for this company include these two statements:

- "On a positive note, *Company* has reduced its carbon emissions from its factories by 7% within the past year"
- "*Company* unfortunately continues to produce non-recyclable containers that contribute to landfills"

These two statements are categorized within the topics of Carbon and Waste, respectively, in the above figure. Additionally, both statements are counted within the aggregated ESG dimensions assessment for this corporation, the first as a positive score and the second as a negative score. The aggregation of scores (such as sentiment) across all applicable statements within all ESG dimensions contributes to an overall score for the Company.

Another requirement for domain-specific analysis relates to sentiment classification. Consider the medical domain and the following two phrases that might realistically come from social media posts:

1. "My cousin heard today she has the disease."
2. "My friend's disease was cured with medication and lifestyle adjustments."

Most people reading these would assign the first phrase a negative sentiment, due to the recent (today) revelation of a disease, an object noun phrase which has negative interpretation. However, reading the second post we would interpret this phrase as a positive sentiment, because it describes a favorable outcome (indicated by "cured"). However, a general purpose, naïve text-mining analysis may assign negative sentiment to both phrases due to the word "disease."

Both open source and commercial developers have built domain specific text processing engines, incorporating specialized dictionaries. One example from Amazon Web Services can process clinical medical documents utilizing the SNOMED dictionary, accepted as an industry standard (Meharizghi et al. 2021).

- Commercial packages

As of this writing, there are a broad range of commercial software packages that analyze social media data streams, and earned media including newswires. These packages include Brandwatch, Quid, Meltwater, Talkwalker, and Netbase, among others, and names of products may change over time due to mergers, acquisition, and re-branding. Collectively these packages can extract topics from documents, cluster documents based on those topics, assign sentiment to individual posts as well as average sentiment across topics. The widespread availability of these packages makes general analyses of sentiment and topic ranking cost effective. However, specific domain taxonomies are required to gain more accurate topic classification and sentiment assignment.

- Custom coding

In addition to using commercial software packages for text mining, some advanced analytics groups have their internal staff write custom code to supplement this. For example, Python code can be written to process longer-form text documents to divide into sub-sections, or to fill specific templates for processing structured documents.

- Machine Learning Classification Engine

Especially when building custom text mining for a particular application domain, it is helpful to utilize a machine-learning environment for classifying text entries with high accuracy. Say you are attempting to classify Twitter posts as positive or negative sentiment in a particular domain like responses to entertainment-related postings. You notice that new vocabulary among younger viewers is making the results misclassified, or introducing too many "zero" or neutral sentiment values.

In such cases, you need to develop a custom algorithm to supplement the commercial software. Taking a traditional classification training approach, follow this procedure:

1. Gather a large training sample of tweets within this entertainment review category.
2. Come up with a feature extraction method to represent each post as a series of model input "fields."
3. Randomly divide into three groups: a training set, a model validation set, and a holdout sample. Ratios might be 60-20-20 by percentage.
4. Score the training set of tweets "manually" as to what the classification should be. This is the most time-consuming step and may benefit from offshoring or partnership with a vendor.
5. Build a classification model based on extracted features from the tweets and using the training and validation samples.
   - Different techniques may be attempted: regression, random forest, neural network, etc.
6. Evaluate the model performance on the holdout sample. For example, if this is a binary classifier, use a confusion matrix to evaluate based on true positive and true negative rates (sensitivity and specificity).

There are vendors available that can assist with this process of customized text mining classifiers. Among those offering text mining classification services for business use are Amazon and IBM Watson.

8.5 Appling Results to Strategy

With the basic elements of topic extraction, sentiment processing, and machine learning in place, how are these packaged into strategic business applications, discussed at the beginning of this chapter? Text mining being an innovative field of business application, there is room for creativity here, but these are two frameworks to apply:

- *Reputation scorecards*: Say you are comparing several competing technology companies on their reputation among key stakeholders, such as business users, and industry media. Aggregated statistics (volume of posts, sentiment scores) across the topics within dimensions can help in calibrating and ranking the brands. See the table below for these basic elements. The data suggest that during the time period of Q2 2022, related to Product Assessment by Business Users, Company B has the highest share of voice (25% more posts than company A) and has the highest net sentiment ranking. There is ample room within this basic framework for companies to vary the metrics, methods of scoring, and visualizations of this scorecard (Table 8.1).
- *Crisis alert monitoring*: If your firm is concerned about public perception and wants to prepare for a possible crisis to respond to, a common scenario is to utilize commercial text mining software and monitor daily mentions of certain related topics mentioned for you or your company. A threshold of negative sentiment mentions for 1 day can trigger an email alert for further review. For example, the issue to monitor may be the safety of your products, and terms to search for as "unsafe," "accident," etc. combined with the product name.

TABLE 8.1 Framework for Reputation Scorecards

Time Period: Q2 2022	Dimension: Products		
Stakeholder: business users	Company A	Company B	Company C
Volume of posts (index)	100	125	87
Net sentiment score	0.45	0.58	−0.22

8.6 Complementing Primary Market Research

Before venturing further, we should acknowledge another core discipline for achieving these business goals, which is primary market research. One can gather the perspectives and opinions of key stakeholders with focus groups, surveys, and interviews, conducted in person, online, or by phone. The respondents are pre-screened to ensure they are eligible and classified correctly within the right cohort. The research results are tabulated, and differences tested for statistical significance. Indeed, this is a good business practice to follow, and there are specific experts to consult for executing these.

However, the text mining approaches we will cover here are complementary to traditional market research, for the following reasons:

- Text mining can be used to discover new topics that may not be anticipated in designing a primary research focus group or survey. For this reason, text mining can be a valuable preceeding step, to identify critical topics that should be probed further in focus groups or surveys.
- Text mining accesses data sources that are a dedicated, less structured environment where stakeholder interactions occur, such as review sites, social media, and article comments. People are more free to express their perspectives in their own terminology, and in a peer-to-peer setting, rather than in interviews.
- Finally, text mining can achieve higher volumes in a more rapid timeframe. Depending on the topic, it is possible to collect and process millions of inputs in a short period of time for popular consumer brands. For more technical, industry-specific studies, hundreds or thousands of responders can be found that otherwise may be difficult to reach.
- Text mining can be more cost effective than conducting a market research study, once automated processes and analytics are established.

Now, the text mining inputs have methodology concerns, like responder bias, and inconsistent language over time. For these reasons, a complete stakeholder assessment should view it as complementary to thorough market research.

8.7 Text Mining Service Applications: Chatbots and Virtual Assistants

In a chapter focused on text mining applications for sales and marketing, we would be remiss if we did not reference two technology trends that blossomed in the 2010s and became mainstream in the 2020s: virtual assistants and chatbots. Both of these are applications of text mining and machine learning and are valuable for sales, customer service, and even as research tools to support new product strategy.

- A virtual assistant is embedded either within computers, mobile phones, or stand-alone, internet-connected devices. They process primarily speech signals, translate them to text, and then either carry out instructions or respond with information. Leading examples are Siri from Apple, Alexa from Amazon, Cortana from Microsoft, or the Google Assistant.

- A chatbot is an assistant embedded within a customer-facing website that can answer product-related questions or assist in searching for information. They have been created for diverse applications, including online retail selling of electronics, insurance sales and claims support, and patient assistance programs in healthcare,

What these two solutions have in common is their utilization of natural language processing, text mining, and predictive modeling. The NLP is clearly needed to translate the input request into a specific command or query, often by filling in a template. However, additionally the context is critical, especially for customer support applications. Consider the following section of a hypothetical chatbot interaction related to purchasing insurance:

> PROSPECTIVE BUYER: I have a question about term life insurance
> CHATBOT: I can help you. What is your age?
> BUYER: 45
> CHATBOT: Do you smoke?
> BUYER: No. How much is the monthly premium?

Now in order to reply, the chatbot has to parse the phrase "monthly premium" and realize that "premium" refers to a noun, not an adjective, and denotes the cost of the life insurance, which was discussed two responses earlier. That number must be retrieved via a table query using the age (45), and (potentially) the number adjusted from say annual to monthly. This can be achieved by different techniques, such as:

- filling in a template related to insurance purchase requests, or
- calculating predictive model probabilities for the word "premium" that infers the correct meaning from other cues.

8.8 Conclusions

This chapter has pointed out the benefits of mining unstructured text for strategic business purposes, including sales, marketing, strategy, and communications objectives. Text mining can supplement traditional market research by capturing conversations and reactions of business stakeholders in their own words. Text mining is an evolving and fascinating field and requires specialized data pre-processing and representation techniques combined with established advanced analytics methods.

8.9 Exercises

1. Describe one of your company's brands or product lines where knowing the opinion of customers is critical.
2. Aside from customers, are there other stakeholders (as listed in this chapter), that are critical for your business to succeed?
   a) How do you gather the assessments and needs of these stakeholders currently?
   b) Are there other general or industry specific data sources that can be analyzed to gather this information?
3. Think of a specialized industry you work in, read about, or comment on, that has text with distinctive jargon which may "confuse" straightforward sentiment classifiers.
   a) How would you attempt to resolve this using machine learning?
   b) Are there specific features of text statements, posts or articles that could help in yielding more accurate classification?

9
PREDICTIVE MODELING FOR BUSINESS

Multivariate predictive modeling is a big data analytics technique that applies merged, integrated data sets to the task of fitting an outcome variable. Mathematically and elegantly stated, the model has the following form:

$$Y = f(\underline{X}) + \varepsilon$$

where $\underline{X} = X_1, X_2 \ldots X_k$ is a vector of k input variables and ε is an error term that is presumed normally distributed with zero mean. The model is determined by a goodness of fit and accuracy to a large array of training data, each data point of which has values for the Xi and the output Y.

More precisely, a *predictive model* most often refers to when the output Y is numeric. Alternatively, the analysis is called a *classification model* when the output Y is the selection of a categorical value, or perhaps the probability assignment among categorical values.

For example, a predictive model may estimate the future annual sales for a retail customer to be $2,000 while a classification model may determine that customer is in the frequent shopper segment.

Classification models are natural extensions of a segmentation project, because a marketer may aim to predict a prospect's most likely segment, before offering terms of a relationship. Another special type of classification model is binary classification, which predicts a True/False relationship. Examples of this are in fraud detection or churn analysis, where you have a relatively low a priori likelihood of the "true" label, but a binary classifier will increase that likelihood and be more accurate in assigning the outcome than random chance. In this chapter, we will cover lessons learned in developing and deploying both predictive models and classification models.

DOI: 10.4324/9780429300363-11

Predictive models have become essential in the business world. At their heart, they aim to calculate an outcome automatically that previously might have been estimated by trained human professionals.

In fact, predictive modeling is tailor-made for sales and marketing applications, as they can be applied to the full customer journey. At any stage of this journey, a company has to indeed predict what a prospect or customer might do next. The models generally can are used as a predictor of likelihood, or alternatively ranking. The applicability of predictive models is akin to this series of assessments:

- I have a prospect or customer at a certain stage.
- If I knew their intentions or their status, I could take certain actions: messaging and touchpoints.
  - Alas, I do not, either due to lack of information, or privacy restrictions.
- However, by using the data available and my predictive model, I can estimate a rank or likelihood they will fit this pattern.
- Based on this model score, I can act accordingly by either activating the touchpoint, or refraining and substituting with another action, or wait.

9.1 Why Predictive Modeling Has Accelerated

Predictive models are applicable where a fairly stable business process is governed by a few numeric thresholds, key performance indicators, or category assignments. Predictive Modeling has accelerated dramatically in business throughout the 2010s and 2020s because the technique is closely tied to automation, scalability, and cost efficiency. Consider these cases in Table 9.1.

In each of these situations, an automated decision can be made based on a straightforward calculation using available customer data, whether on the membership application, recent behavioral transactions, or other stored account

TABLE 9.1 Business Applications of Predictive Models

Business Scenario	Predictive Model	Action Taken if Score Above Threshold
Digital advertising	Likely product purchaser	Serve ads to devices of most likely
Granting a loan to a new auto purchaser	Credit score, likelihood of reliable payment	Grant credit, rate and amount depending on score
Sending a credit offer	Likelihood to respond, plus credit worthiness	Send direct mail with credit card solicitation
Customer service	Likelihood for attrition	Provide additional support and offers to avoid customer churn.

profile fields. The decision no longer requires a human financial representative or customer service agent.

This promise of accuracy and consistency, along with potential savings through automating typically manual processes, is what has driven the accelerated adoption of predictive models.

9.2 Business Stages for Successful Predictive Modeling

Successful predictive modeling requires four equally important phases, spelled out in Figure 9.1, and to be explored in some depth here.

- *Problem Formulation*: Here is where an analytics leader must frame the business problem as either a functional mathematical relationship or a category assignment. Recall our first chapter and the importance of making that translation.

Subsequently, there should be endorsement at the company or the client that such a model is worth pursuing for possibly changing a business process. Seek this endorsement from at least one marketing, sales, or operations leader, while managing expectations about time required to develop models and uncertainty of success.

After the problem has been formulated, take stock of what data sources are available: customer attributes, affiliations and networks, and behavioral transactions. Investigate the methodology behind each data source, along with time-span and update frequency.

- *Data Engineering*: It has been an off-cited adage that for any major analytics project, 80% of the efforts is spent in data management and processing, or in the more inclusive and modern term: data engineering. This stage includes ETL (extract, transformation, load) processes to stand-up input files in a secure, cloud-based analytical environment supporting general purpose data science tools such as Python, R, and SQL, as well as one or more data visualization packages.

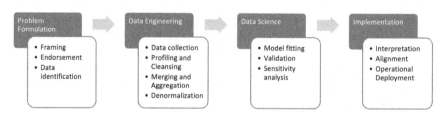

FIGURE 9.1 Stages of Predictive Modeling

Once files are loaded, they should be profiled for field distributions and quality checked for missing values, outliers, expected counts, and other tests as applicable. If required, imputation methods can fill in missing values. If passing quality tests, then data engineering includes filtering, querying, and joining tables as appropriate to support predictive analytics.

Databases for sales and marketing applications are usually set up in a relational structure, with dimension tables (e.g. customer, category, geography) and fact tables (e.g. purchase transactions). This is recommended for storage efficiency, modularity, and maintenance. However, for predictive analytics often a "sandbox" environment is created for model development. The sandbox contains denormalized tables with aggregations at the customer level, just as we discussed in our chapter on segmentation.

- *Data Science*: This is the stage of actually creating the models. Best practice is to separate data into training, testing, and validation samples, as shown conceptually in Figure 9.2. Typical ratios are 60% training, 30% testing, and 10% validation. For forecasting models that aim to predict future trends, the validation set is best chosen for a future time period.

The modeling process should follow these steps:

1. Starting with the training set, utilize up to several techniques (see next major section) to determine which has the best goodness of fit in explaining variation in Y outputs among the training data. We will cover goodness of fit metrics later in this chapter.
2. Then apply the best fitting model forms to observations in the testing data set and again check for fit among the output Y. This evaluation on the testing set is to avoid overfitting of the analysis on the training data set.

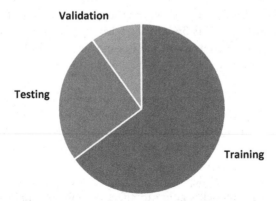

FIGURE 9.2 Dividing Up Modeling Data Set into (from Right, then Clockwise): Training, Testing, and Validation

If the performance on the testing data set shows marked degradation or unacceptable results, then iteration among these two steps is necessary.

3. Once one or more acceptable models are found on both training and testing sets, then apply the model forms to the validation data set for an additional goodness of fit check. Note this is especially important for future-looking forecasting models, where the validation data set should be in a future time period.

A technique that embeds validation within the model fitting process is called *K-fold cross-validation*. The training data set is divided into K equal sections, and then for K iterations, (K−1) of the sections are used to fit a predictive model, with the Kth section used for validation. Then either the optimal model or a blend can be chosen for further evaluation. The benefit of cross-validation is decreasing the likelihood of overfitting on a particular training set.

Once validated, a model should be evaluated with sensitivity analysis to understand how a small change in critical, dynamic input variables will affect the prediction or classification. Here is an example: You are building a model to predict likelihood of credit card default, as a function of customer demographics, total spend, and outstanding balance. Your input data set has a limited range for those quantitative variables; say total spend in your inputs varies from $0 to $950. Your prediction may fit well within those ranges, but what is predicted should the total spend rise to $1,500, $2,000, or higher?

- *Implementation* This stage is critical to have a completed analytical model actually make an impact on a business process. First, you have to interpret the results. What are the implications of this validated model, and what business decisions will the company make as a result of this model? That leads to an alignment issue: determining if your business is comfortable with these decisions and their consequences, and allocating associated resources. Take, for example, a customer support call center. If a binary classification model predicts 3% of callers have potential for churn (lapsing) and require special attention or offers, can your firm dedicate staffing time to address those issues?

Then finally the implementation includes operational deployment, which is embedding the predictive model within corporate systems to run reliably and at scale. Another term for this is machine learning operations, or ML Ops. Specialized programing tools exist for compiling and exporting validated models for use in production environments.

Part of the operational deployment goes beyond technology and into human factors. If your model is going to affect the jobs of employees like sales representatives or call center counselors, then training and transparency are critical. Analytics leaders must prepare written, readily accessible materials on the predictive model's intent, basic functionality, and outputs. There should be explanations and discussions of how and what decisions are made for each output, whether the decisions are made automatically or with human judgment. This educational effort will be most valuable in building trust and in allowing for backup planning.

9.3 Common Predictive Modeling Techniques

In this section, we will provide a general overview of a range of the most commonly employed predictive modeling techniques within sales and marketing. Each technique will be described generally with comments on applicability to business problems. We will also provide references to other texts that go deeper into the methodology for each.

9.3.1 Statistical Regression

In statistical multivariate regression, the model is predicting a numerical variable

$$Y = f(\underline{\mathbf{X}}) = a_1 X_1 + a_2 X_2 + \cdots + a_k X_k + \varepsilon$$

The coefficients a_i are determined by ordinary least squares minimization over the training data set. Details are provided in Freund and Wilson (1998) and Dillon and Goldstein (1984).

As characterized in the above equation, this is considered a *linear regression*. On some occasions, a nonlinear transformation is applied to one or more of the X_i either for business causal reasons or to equilibrate the scales of the different factors. One example is taking a logarithm transformation of an input like media impressions in the millions to be at the same scale of other input factors.

When the Y and the X_i also indexed by consecutive time periods (say weekly, monthly, quarterly), then this formulation is a *time-series regression*. One application of time-series regression is Marketing Mix Modeling, which is a macro-level analysis of the contribution of multiple media channels in determining sales trends. See Hanssens (2015) for details and an edited compendium of this application, as well as (Wei 2005). See Haimowitz et al (1995) for a combined time series and AI-based approach to modeling.

9.3.2 Logistic Regression

Logistic regression is a specialized case of statistical regression that is used for predicting the probability P (between 0 and 1) of an outcome that is often somewhat rare. Business examples are predicting the probability of customer attrition, fraud detection, credit defaults, or a patient having a disease, In this case, the Y outcome of the regression formula is replaced by the logit function:

$$\text{Logit}\left[P\right] = \text{Ln}\left[P / (1 - P)\right] = a_1 X_1 + a_2 X_2 + \ldots + a_k X_k + \in$$

The result of fitting this model is that all observations are assigned a probability of the predicted event. Observations can then be sorted and compared to actuals for validation in a lift curve, as we will describe later in this chapter.

9.3.3 Time Series Forecasting

Another statistical predictive modeling technique is *time series forecasting*. A primary business example is category forecasting within packaged goods, expressing future quarterly sales as a function of prior sales. Time series forecasting has a foundation of matching patterns over time to two primary types of components:

- *autoregressive*: each value is a weighted average of prior values over a window, and
- *moving average*: a weighted average of a normally distributed, mean-centered series over another window.

An ARMA(p, q) model that sums these components has the functional form:

$$Y_t = C + a_1 \times Y_{t-1} + \ldots + a_p \times Y_{t-p} + e_t - b_1 \times e_{t-1} - \ldots - b_q \times e_{t-q}$$

The first portion of this formula is the autoregressive component, and the second half is the moving average of normally distributed random variables. There is a *stationary* assumption of an ARMA model for a time series, which in business terms means no major systemic shifts.

As an example, Figure 9.3 shows 6 months of weekly univariate data fitting an ARMA(1,1) series, where C= 7, a_1= 0.3, and b_1 = −0.7.

FIGURE 9.3 Auto-Regressive Moving Average ARMA(1,1) Time Series

Adding a non-stationary component (as seen in seasonality, or market expansion) results in an ARIMA time series; the I stands for "integrated." They are related so that an ARIMA (p, 0, q) model is the same as an ARMA(p, q) model.

From a business perspective, fitting the ARIMA model enables sales projections for the next several time periods, which can be checked on a validation data set of future values occurring after the training and testing data sets. Beyond pure univariate ARIMA, the next level of complexity is time-series-based multivariate regression, where a series like weekly sales is a function not only of auto-regressive and moving average effects but also other causal variables including price, promotion levels, and items in the store. For an in-depth treatment of ARIMA time-series models and their extensions, and how to solve for the parameters in applied forecasting, see Makridakis et al. (1998).

9.3.4 Neural Networks

A neural network is a predictive model that fits non-linear relationships and is based on weighted connections between nodes (or units), similar conceptually to neurons in the brain. Figure 9.4 shows a conceptual example of a neural network with an input layer (shaded) on left for loading the inputs X and an output layer shaded on right for calculating one or more outputs Y. In between are middle layers of nodes; the number of middle layers and nodes per layer are configurable.

The connections between nodes are governed by weights Wij that propagate signal s from a node in one layer to the next. Calculation of an output from a middle or output layer j consists of two stages:

1. Compute a *net input,* Ij which is weighted average of the inputs from the previous layer's inputs, plus a bias:

$$I_j = \sum \{w_{ij} \times O_i\} + B_j$$

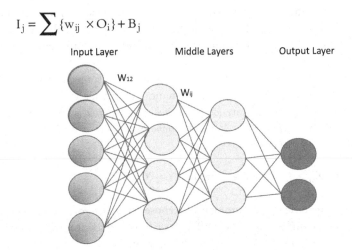

FIGURE 9.4   A Multi-Layer Neural Network

where the Oi are the outputs from the I units that feed into the calculating unit, and Bj is a bias of the unit.

2 Feed Ij into a logistic, or sigmoid function to compute the output of unit j:

$$O_j = 1 / (1 + e^{-Ij})$$

In this way, outputs for each layer are calculated forward to the output layer, where results are compared to the actual Y values of the training data set. The model parameters are adjusted via a *backpropagation* algorithm, which iteratively adjusts the weights in order to optimize the predictive accuracy of the neural network on the training data set.

Detailed instructions of neural network computation can be found in Han and Kamber (2006) as well as in Duda et al. (2001). Neural networks have desirable properties of ability to fit nonlinear data and perform well on validation data even somewhat outside the training data ranges. The chief drawback of neural network has been its difficulty to concisely explain the input factors driving performance, a property some call a "black box." While once computationally expensive, neural networks have dramatically increased in utilization due to advances in cloud computing, parallel processing, and more usable implementation within the Python language.

9.3.5 Decision Trees and Random Forests

Tree-based models are attractive in providing fairly accurate performance and being explainable in a way similar to "if-then" business rules. A *regression tree* predicts a numerical value, whereas a *classification tree* predicts a distribution of segments. An example regression tree is illustrated in Figure 9.5. One starts at the root of the tree, which represents all observations, and has an average Y value of Y0. The population is then iteratively split and partitioned into two or more subsegments that maximize the difference in the Y output.

In the figure, there are splits into both two and three groups, utilizing each of the inputs X1 to X5. Inputs may be chosen more than once as split variables. Shaded cells in the figure indicate *leaf nodes, which have actual predicted Y values based on the combination of selections at all splits from the top. For example, the rule for the leaf node at the right bottom is:*

$$X_1 > a_1 \text{ and } X_3 > a_2 \text{ and } X_5 > a_3 \text{ predicts } Y = Y'$$

where the a_i are specific values automatically chosen by the algorithm that seeks to locally optimize differences in Y. Different criteria include information gain metrics and significance of a chi-squared distribution.

N Cases, Y = Y0

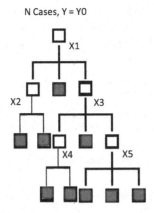

FIGURE 9.5 Decision Tree Based Predictive Model

The full predictive model consists of the "rules" such as above across all leaf nodes of the tree. Regression and classification trees have a drawback of having "stair step" behavior that can limit the accuracy of predictions. An often-used generalization of tree models is a *random forest* in which multiple trees are combined for enabling significant error reduction, although dramatically increasing the leaves and resulting rule sets. For more details and Python programming samples, see Hartshorn (2016).

9.4 Goodness of Fit Measures

How can one tell whether a predictive model fit is sufficient for a business applications? There are multiple possible goodness of fit measures, depending on the model construct and application. Another term for these quantitative measures is loss functions, because the predictive model algorithm aims to minimize these values as they iterate through the algorithm. Typically, these measures are applied as scores on the testing or validation portions of data to measure model effectiveness.

9.4.1 Numerical Predictor Evaluation

- *Percentage of Variation Explained*: This is the R-squared from statistics that is based on how well the model's predicted Y values explain the observed differences of the training data's Y values from its mean. The value is on a 0 to 1 scale; having an R-squared of 0.6 or higher should be a minimal requirement for deployment, and a value of 0.8 or higher is preferred. A value lower than 0.7 really indicates that you may need to include other input variables.

- *Root Mean Squared Error*: This is a metric minimized by statistical regression models. RMSE is expressed below, is positive by definition, and approximates the average distance between predicted and actual values.

$$RMSE = SQRT \{1 / N \times \sum (predicted - actual)^2\}$$

- *Mean Absolute Percentage Error*: MAPE is used for predictions of a numeric variable and is especially valuable for forecasting a series of future values. This calculation for N observations is as follows:

$$MAPE = (1 / N) \times \sum | predicted - actual| / |actual|$$

MAPE will be a positive number, expressed as an average percentage difference (in absolute terms) between the predicted and the actual. The value is non-negative, and for well-fitting models have a value much less than one. However, MAPE can be well above one for predictions that poorly estimate actual values. In several business applications, I have accepted a MAPE level of up to 20%. There is not a universal upper threshold for an acceptable MAPE; rather it is best to compare the MAPE of your model to see if that percentage is lower than that of a very simple model, say that guesses a constant value or an average value from the past.

9.4.2 Classifier Evaluation

- *Lift curve*: A lift curve is ranking-based, and measures the success over a random assignment for a model that predicts a binary variable, particularly a low-percentage outcome or rare event like fraud, credit failure, or a rare disease. Consider, for example, a logistic regression model that calculates the likelihood of a consumer to default on their credit within 6 months, and computes a score from 0 to 1,000; with the lower score being a more probable credit default. Say the model was applied to 100,000 consumers using inputs from January to June, and July to December of the same year was held out as a "future" validation sample. During this validation period, 1,500 consumers actually defaulted, for a 1.5% rate, indeed a low percentage.

On the chart of Figure 9.3, we plot on the horizontal axis the scores from 0 to 1,000 and on the vertical axis the cumulative percent of credit default cases that are correctly predicted with consumers less than or equal to that score. That curve (solid line) increases sharply at the low scores as disproportionately many consumers were correctly predicted. The dotted line represents a uniform distribution of defaulters across scores.

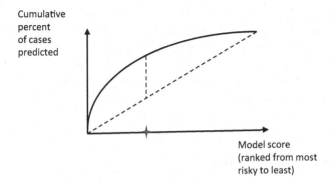

FIGURE 9.6   Figure for a Predictive Model Lift Curve

Let's say that at a score of 300, the predictive model finds 65% of the consumers who ended up defaulting. The uniform score assumption would have 30% of defaulters identified, since 300/1,000 = 30%. The difference of 65% to 30% is a 35% lift at the score of 300. That is represented in Figure 9.6 by the tick-mark on the X-axis and the corresponding difference shown by the vertical line.

In a similar way, an analyst can decide upon different thresholds to see which produces the maximal lift. Indeed, an "area under the curve" (AUC) metric can integrate over the difference between the model output curve and the uniform distribution. This AUC can be used as a model success criterion as well.

• Classification Matrix

A classification matrix evaluates the performance of a classification model that assigns observations to one of a series of groups. The objective is to evaluate what percentage of the time the correct assignment is made, and how often there is an erroneous assignment.

Consider Table 9.2 which reflects the validation outcomes of a classification model to predict next quarter's future shopping behavior of a currently brand-loyal shopper within a competitive environment. There are three segments as options: dormant (minimal purchasing), loyalist (continued brand purchasing primarily), and switcher (significant purchasing with competitive products).

TABLE 9.2 Classification Matrix for a Categorical Predictive Model

	Actual Segment		
Predicted Segment	Dormant	Loyalist	Switcher
Dormant	**1,000**	200	50
Loyalist	125	**300**	100
Switcher	75	100	**250**

The table reflects the predicted future quarterly segments of 2,000 custom-ers validated against the next 3 months of sales data. The correctly assigned segments are **bold font** and indicated in the diagonal.

In this example, the overall percentage correct equals 1,550 / 2,200 = 70.5%.

This may seem like an acceptable prediction, but, in fact, the behavior is driven by the Dormant prediction, correct 80% of the time. The other segments have worse behavior, and we consider those consequences in the exercises at the end of the chapter.

- **Sensitivity and Specificity**

These are particular outcome metrics that are utilized when your model is predicting a binary outcome, namely presence or absence of a transactional condition. This situation is worthy of a separate suite of metrics due to its per-vasiveness, including medical diagnosis, fraud detection, security screening, and credit risk evaluation. All of these are trying to predict fairly rare events. Consider the following table with outcomes from a fictitious small-scale binary classification model that predicted future customer churn away from a monthly phone subscription for 5,000 customers, and 3 months later, the actual cus-tomer status was evaluated (Table 9.3).

Let's use this table to define the core metrics of evaluating binary classifiers:

- There are 100 actual *positive* cases (the left column).
- The *true positive rate (TPR) reflects those actual positive cases where the prediction was also true.* The TPR is thus 75/100 = 75%.
  - The true positive rate is also called the *sensitivity*.
- Similarly, the *true negative rate (TNR) reflects those actual negative cases where the prediction was also negative.* The TNR is thus 4,550/4,900 = 93%.
  - The true negative rate is also called the *specificity*.

Also noteworthy, especially in alarming or testing with major consequences, is the *false positive rate (FPR),* or the portion of all negatives that are incorrectly pre-dicted as positive. In this simple case, the false positive rate is 350 / 4,900 = 7%. Note from these definitions that

$$FPR = 1 - TNR = 1 - Specificity$$

TABLE 9.3 Example Binary Classification Outcomes Table

Predicted churn	Actual Churn	
	Positive	Negative
Positive	75	350
Negative	25	1,550

Finally, the precision is the portion of the positive predictions that are correct, meaning actually positive. In this case, the precision is *75/425 = 18%*.

Now, consider the trade-offs suggested by these metrics and this churn predictor example in the table.

- Our model's True Positive Rate of 75% suggests that implementing this model would let us catch three-quarters of the churn customers in advance, a helpful prospect.
- However, since the precision of the classifier is only 18%, that means that 72% of the time this classifier suggests churn, the model will be incorrect.
- Might it be possible to build a more "aggressive classifier" to catch even more of the churn customers early, say increasing the TPR to 80% or higher? The challenge is that the new classifier may have a lower sensitivity, introduce more false positives, and lower the precision even further.

9.4.3 ROC Curves

Now, say you are building a binary classifier predictive model where the Positive or Negative prediction is determined by a case exceeding some threshold, such as the score of a logistic regression model. Each threshold value is in itself a classifier, which results in a sensitivity and a specificity. A *receiver operating characteristic (ROC) curve* is a graphical plot for the series of connected classifiers varying only by such a parameter value. See Figure 9.7, for example, for a conceptual illustration that plots TPR on the horizontal and FPR on the vertical axes. The shape of the curve demonstrates the trade-off between sensitivity and specificity. At the extreme, if a classifier has a high TPR near 100% that algorithm is likely to also have significant true positives and also miss true

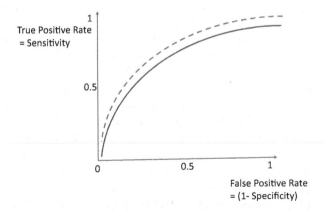

FIGURE 9.7   ROC Curve with Comparing Performance Tradeoff for Two Classifier Models

negatives, making the FPR also high. The sweet spot of the algorithm is where there is fairly high sensitivity and specificity.

Two binary classification algorithms can be compared to each other by comparing their ROC curves. In the figure, the dashed line algorithm is superior, since for the same TPR there is a lower FPR, meaning a higher sensitivity. In fact, one can compute a clever summary metric called AUC, for the area under the curve that rates the binary classification algorithm based on how much area, with a maximum of 1.0 indicating a theoretically maximal algorithm. A 45-degree line has an AUC of 50% and indicates a poor, near random modeling technique.

9.5 Implementation Considerations

A validated predictive model is a candidate for implementation within production business processes. I have personally implemented learning systems within direct mail programs, relationship marketing systems, field force automation platforms, financial bidding algorithms, and credit card offer generators. Along the way, several lessons became apparent on what is required for successful deployment.

- *Transparency*: Before sales executives or product managers will endorse analytics decision-making, they must feel comfortable that the methodology is consistent with their business practice, and that the predictions have been properly validated and hence the need for transparency and clear validation output.
- *Staff Education and Training*: If your deployment supports human decision-making, then training with clear instructions must be provided to those who are experts in their role, but likely not familiar with big data analytics. What does a sales representative do when a client is in the "switcher" segment? What guidance or offers should a call center operator provide when a "possible churn or abandonment" message appears? A good implementation leaves nothing to chance.
- *False Positive and False Negative Tolerances*: It's important when implementing binary classifiers, to consider your corporate or department policies when choosing exactly where on the ROC curve to define your production classifier. How aggressively do you want to catch positive cases of fraud or churn, and how willing are you to tolerate false positive alerts? We explore this in one of the exercises at end of the chapter.
- *Financial Impact Calculations*: Classification threshold decisions can be assisted with realistic quantitative simulations. What is the financial benefit of a retained customer that otherwise would be lost? What is the cost to your business of a false positive risk assessment, in terms of lost customer satisfaction and loyalty? Incorporate these financial parameters and simulate over the expected near-term transactions, to quantify the expected benefits.

- *Refresh Frequency*: Predictive models are developed based on historical data, and as time passes in a dynamic market, those data may not reflect the new business reality. Develop a periodic cycle for validating existing models on more recent transactions and refreshing as needed to improve accuracy. In sales and marketing, this may be a quarterly, semi-annual or annual cycle, depending on category volatility.

- *Analytics Deployment Environments*: As machine learning practitioners and predictive modeling have gained traction across industries, so too has the creation of programmer environments that support scalable model development and deployment. These have started as opensource coding communities that were later enhanced, sponsored, and supported by leading technology firms. As an example, TensorFlow is an open source Python software library for machine intelligence, released by Google in the mid-2010s. This has been supplemented by Keras, an API interface for supporting model prototyping. Additionally, Kubernetes is a compatible series of tools for deploying machine-learning models within industrial software applications. Good resources for getting started are found in Burns et al. (2019) and Geron (2019), but these should be supplemented by active blogs, podcasts, and conferences, to monitor the rapid innovations in these environments.

9.6 Conclusions

In this chapter, we have provided a general overview of predictive modeling within a commercial business environment. We started with the motivations for intelligent, data-driven prediction, and described the business processes for modeling. Then after reviewing the leading types of predictive models, we offered guidance as to how to judge the accuracy of predictors, whether classifiers or quantitative estimators. Finally, we concluded with important principles for implementing these analytic models within a production business environment.

9.7 Exercises

1. You are building a predictive model for a telecommunications carrier to predict whether an existing customer may churn (switch suppliers) within the next 3 months. The goal is to use this model with customer service agents to determine whether to change the standard call script and offer financial incentives to stay. Your guidelines from management are that your model when validated should predict 7% of customers having churn, while having at least a 95% true positive rate and no more than a 10% false negative rate.

   a) At these exact specifications, for every 1,000 customers reaching your call center, how many would be judged to have a churn prediction.

   b) Of those, how many would be correctly identified for churn? Incorrectly?

   c) How many of these 1,000 customers would be incorrectly missed and leave your company?

2. Consider the profile of the classification model in the shopping example given in Table 9.2.

   a) Which of your segment predictions has the worst performance, measured by correct classification rate?

   b) Say the cost of failing to classify a switcher is $500 per customer. If the model is applied to the next 100,000 customers, how much revenue (in the worst case) could be lost due to such misclassification?

   c) Say you offer a $50 discount to all customers you predict could be switchers to retain their business. How much lost revenue would that result in due to misclassification of loyalists as switchers?

3. Consider the binary classification results in Table 9.3, which are said to be satisfactory based on 5,000 validation cases for a basic customer retention problem. How would you feel about these results in each of the three cases below? What particular statistic (by name) would you wish to improve and why? What are the applicable trade-offs and costs associated with each problem:

   a) Airline security screening, where a "positive" is a flight security risk requiring a closer manual inspection.

   b) Oncology screening, where a "positive" is a risk for cancer requiring more detailed in-hospital testing.

   c) Choose a business application in your company with an important Yes/No binary classification.

PART III

Implementation and Delivery

10

PRIVACY CONSIDERATIONS FOR BIG DATA ANALYTICS

10.1 Concerns Related to Data Privacy

As discussed in the prior chapters, the past 20 years have brought seismic advances in data sources, integration, analytics methods, and business operations. All of these have contributed to enhanced pervasiveness of intelligence-driven marketing and sales based on customer behaviors and other background data, especially in the rapid-response, addressable digital channels like paid search, display, and online video advertising and email. Additionally, even television advertising has become personalized to the household level, with targeting possible due to purchase-based segments.

While many businesses have leveraged and benefitted from these assets, there has also been a backlash from customers who do not wish to have their private behavioral data utilized, even for marketing purposes. Websites in U.S. now regularly communicate to new visitors how they utilize cookies, seeking approval before pages are shown. A recent 2021 study by Cisco of over 2,600 adults in 12 countries found that "eighty-six percent of respondents cared about their data privacy and want more control, while 79% were willing to act by not making a purchase, expecting to pay more for privacy, and spending money to protect their data" (Vigliarolo 2021). Other studies have found a mixed consumer response (McDonald 2018; Neufeld 2017).

These findings have consequences for companies leveraging integrated data assets for sales and marketing purposes. In this chapter, we will first review the core methodologies of how consumer identities are utilized for the core marketing processes of targeting and measurement. With that foundation, we will then list several public policies and corporate reactions to those mechanisms. We conclude with how the big data analytics practices have been

DOI: 10.4324/9780429300363-13

reacting to maintain their marketing capabilities despite the changing regulatory and marketplace environment.

10.2 Core Processes Leveraging Consumer Data

This section will describe the mechanisms by which consumer data is leveraged for both targeting and measurement. Fundamentally, the data connectivity required for these processes is bi-directional, and illustrated in Figure 10.1. As noted at the left, a consumer may connect to the internet using several devices, such as a laptop computer, mobile phone, or tablet. For one or more of the websites visited, that consumer may provide personal credentials and permission as part of a registration process. He or she may provide:

- *Personally identifiable information*, such as name, address, email, or phone number. This is provided in order to receive access to information, or follow-up communications.
- *Permission* for marketing, according to the privacy policy of the website publisher or underlying business that provides the goods and services. The privacy policy can often allow use of a consumer's information for marketing purposes.

Now given that the consumer accesses the internet with multiple devices, a company at the heart of digital marketing is an *identity resolution partner*. Such a company maintains a *device graph* that updates records for different technology devices as connected to each other and connected to the person that supplied his or her identifiable information.

In the figure, if the consumer logs into a website with identification credentials using another device, then the identity resolution partner can establish a connection between those devices. In this way, the device graph is maintained and updated over time as users acquire more digital devices and establish identities across logged-in, permission-based websites.

In addition, there is another function that identity resolution partners can perform, and that is of a haven for matching consumer identities to external

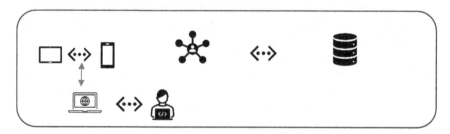

FIGURE 10.1 Identity Resolution Processes

databases of marketing firms that are not allowed to possess consumer identifiable information. This is represented in the right side of the figure above. The company in effect creates a table that matches, or links, a consumer identity to an identifier in the external database. The matching is accomplished through a series of anonymized hash keys, or encryption functions, so that the identity cannot be fully recovered. The resulting table has been referred to as a crosswalk file, or a bridge file, given its linking nature.

A closely related concept to digital identity resolution is the usage of *cookies,* or small text files written to a device indicating that a user has visited a particular website or seen a particular advertisement. *First-party cookies* are placed on a device by a website to improve that user's experience on future website visits, as with personalized content. Increasingly, websites ask permission on dialogue boxes to first-time visitors to place cookies on that device. *Third-party cookies* are placed by other entities such as advertising services, for either customized digital targeting, or digital media measurement. An ad service can know that a user's device is a potential fit for a campaign based on prior cookies left by evidence of relevant site visits, or views of prior targeted ads based on demographics or purchase segments. The next section describes the steps of behavioral targeting in more detail. Afterwards, we will discuss promotional measurement and data privacy considerations.

10.2.1 Behavioral Targeting Considerations

First let's consider the use case of behavioral targeting, which is serving a promotion or advertisement to consumers based on prior purchase history. An example of this might be a manufacturer of salty snacks packaged goods who wishes to target people or households with a history of purchasing pretzels, snack chips, or peanuts within the past year. Re-examining Figure 10.1, we see that the direction of information flow is from right to left: from purchase behaviors to media-enabled devices.

For this use case, there are a few considerations:

- On some occasions, a user may have explicitly given permission to receive advertising communications as they registered for a loyalty or CRM program with this company or one of its brands. In that case, direct communications can be sent.
- In most cases, the consumer has not provided explicit permission to receive advertisements. Therefore, in light of the current climate, an advertiser cannot directly communicate based on purchase. While we are talking about packaged goods and salty snacks in this example, this is relevant also to far more sensitive in domains like healthcare. As a result, to preserve privacy, the ads must be sent to a broader set of consumers that are likely

to have a purchase history. In this way, advertising can strike a balance between:

- having a lift of targeted reach over the general broadcast of demographic-based advertising and
- preserving consumer privacy.

Industry trade groups in the US such as the National Advertising Initiative (NAI) have been created, in part, to promote guidelines for preserving consumer privacy, including how broad the targeted set must be, specific to industries.

Using the apparatus in Figure 10.1, an advertiser can first determine which of the consumers in their database fits the desirable pattern to target. This might be the consumers who are trying the category for the first time, or who are using a competitive brand. The analog in pharmaceuticals is patients who are diagnosed with the relevant disease but treating on a competitive drug. To preserve privacy, the marketer must then generalize the data set of those targeted, using big data analytics techniques as we have described in our chapter on Targeting. Once the selected target set of consumers is chosen, the coded identifiers are sent to the identity resolution firm. That firm can then map back to the digital devices (or household television accounts) that match, so that the ads can be placed on those devices and reach the targets. The specifics of how the ads are served depend on the channel, the media agencies, and trading desks involved.

When cookies are utilized, the targeted ads can become increasingly based on prior website visitation or purchase models. In principle, this is providing more customized advertising to users of products they would find relevant; however, consumers may feel these unexpected ads are too personal and off-putting. More details on recent trends with cookies are discussed later in this chapter.

10.2.2 Marketing Measurement Considerations

The dual use case to behavioral targeting is promotional measurement. The general principle is to measure the effectiveness of a marketing campaign by seeing how it drives consumers further along the customer journey to purchase, and even to loyalty. Marketers want to measure the effectiveness of advertising programs, across media channels and touchpoints. This is important for media budget optimization: re-allocating spend across channels and tactics.

For example, consider the marketplace for consumer packaged goods, or other retail purchased products. A marketing firm that has a longitudinal consumer purchase transactional database, such as loyalty card data, wishes to measure the impact of digital media campaigns. As with the targeting use case, there are two cases to consider:

- If the promoted consumers are all registered with permission for a relationship marketing program, then these consumers are retrievable by name and are directly matchable to the program database, for measurement of incremental purchase (say via redeemed coupons) by promotional channel.
- Alternatively, the consumers getting advertising impressions are not registered but are anonymous. In this case, we return to Figure 10.1 and read the processing from left to right. The exposed devices that viewed the ad are collected by the identity resolution vendor and merged using the device graph. Those individuals are then matched using the crosswalk file to the marketing company's transactional database, for measurement of incremental purchase.

Recall in Chapter 7 on campaign measurement we discussed multi-touch attribution which links ad exposures anonymously to particular customer behaviors that affect sales, especially in the off-line world of retail, including car dealerships, supermarkets, and pharmacy chains, depending on the business industry performing the measurement.

10.3 Privacy-Related Policies

10.3.1 Government Legislation

In the late 2010s, an array of privacy legislation was enacted by governments to limit the use of consumer information for business purposes by third parties. The most stringent of these has been the General Data Protection Regulation (GDPR), enacted by the European Union in 2016 and put into effect in May 2018. The GDPR explicitly limited the collection and usage of consumer-level data without clear permission, which limited dramatically the availability of such data.

In the US, there is no such federal law imposing restrictions on consumer privacy, although there are several industry specific guidelines such as the Health Insurance Portability and Accountability Act (HIPAA) for restricting healthcare data sharing and the Gramm-Leach-Bliley Act (GLBA) for transparency about disclosure of consumer financial data. As of this writing, there are also state-specific regulations in three states (California, Virginia, Colorado) that restrict data usage for residents (Klosowski 2021); such restrictions may be expanding over time.

10.3.2 Privacy Policies of Technology Corporations

Concurrent with these government policies, private corporations in the internet technology space began taking actions to preserve their image as protectors of privacy. The primary step taken has been through elimination of use of third-party cookies within their website browsers. Apple has implanted intelligent tracking prevention with increasing privacy features in the late 2010s, and Google has announced its Chrome browser will not support third-party cookies at some point in 2024.

The consequences of these government and technology firm restrictions have meant an increased reliance on first-party cookies and usage of permission-based data in both advertising and measurement. The consequence of this shift is becoming reduced match rates for both targeting and measurement, at least until levels of consumer permissions reaches reach a critical threshold.

10.4 Data Integration and Certification

To protect consumer privacy, several leading data vendors with transactional behavior assets containing personally identifiable information will anonymize their data sets when licensing that data for marketing research. The types of studies these anonymized data sets support are analysis of sales trends and understanding patterns in a customer's journey.

When two such vendors wish to match data to create a combined research asset, they often perform a process called *tokenization* that merges combinations of several fields together with hash keys, or computed codes. The series of hash keys are chosen to give high quality matching results. Often, a separate third-party "clean room" vendor performs the matching, so that neither data vendor can see the others' PII attributes.

A combined data set, even if anonymized, should go through a certification to demonstrate a near-zero chance of reverse reidentification from the merge, and related analytic reporting. Specialized firms and consultants can perform these assessments using statistical calculations and by understanding the reporting use cases of the research using this merged data. To play it safe, consider reporting research results at a general enough level to leave no chance of identifying individual consumers. Hypothetical examples:

- Males over 45 in California have a higher risk rate of this disease than the general population
- Females over 30 in the Northeast on average use consumer credit frequently for apparel.

The data sets alluded to are in the thousands to tens of thousands, and so provide no possibility to interpret individuals

10.5 Conclusions

In this chapter, we have provided an overview of the growing consumer privacy environment and their implications for sales and marketing. Far more restrictions are in place in Europe for consumer (and professional) data collection.

However, especially for consumers, privacy concerns in the US are increasing and leading to permission-based frameworks to take a more prominent role in both targeting and measurement. The landscape of consumer privacy and marketing guidelines is quite dynamic, and the reader is advised to stay apprised via trade press, associations, blogs, and communities in the relevant industries and media channels.

10.6 Exercises

1. Find a published survey of consumer privacy attitudes in your industry and local market, that spells out feelings toward sharing personal information in exchange for customized marketing or services.
   a) What findings do you notice regarding consumers privacy concerns?
   b) How do these compare to 3–5 years ago?
   c) What are the implications for market research analysis in your industry?
   d) What are the implications for personalized targeting and communications?
2. You run an online retail website with hundreds of products across apparel, accessories, and home goods. A high percentage of consumers have accepted your first-party cookies. Thus, you can tell what repeat site visitors have purchased before.
   a) When repeat visitors come back 1 week after buying an expensive apparel item, what products would you feature on their home page?
   b) Is the above strategy clearly answered, or one you would test into?
   c) How would this answer change if the user has not visited your website for 6 months?

11

DELIVERING RESULTS WITH ACTIONABLE INSIGHTS

Say your company has worked so diligently to build capabilities around data engineering and advanced analytics, and is now generating novel and insightful results. The next stage is to make these findings applicable to drive real business change at either your internal matrixed departments, or your clients if your firm is a service provider. In this chapter, we will cover the best methods to deliver big data results to achieve measurable business impact.

The outputs such as predictive models, segments, or patterns ultimately must be understood, validated, and implemented within a business process. This chapter will account for several lessons such as utilization of self-service dashboards, the benefits of data visualization, the value of storytelling to highlight the insights, and directly feeding big data output into an automated operational process. We will illustrate these concepts with three case studies: media optimization, sales force effectiveness, and competitive intelligence.

11.1 Dimensions of Analytics Delivery

One critical set of decisions an analytics organization must make is how to deliver results and insights to clients. The nature of these decisions can define the reputation of your group, and the utility of the offerings. If your group is on the supplier side, these choices will dictate the commercial value of your output, which in turn can move you up on the price vs. value equation.

Let's articulate the dimensions of analytics delivery. Then we can evaluate alternative scenarios that your organization may adopt, based on specific points along these dimensions. We will evaluate the pros and cons of each alternative, to help you make a decision on how to move forward.

DOI: 10.4324/9780429300363-14

- *Business Model*: The most fundamental categorization of analytics delivery is whether the business model is a *product* or a *service*. In a product-based delivery, outputs are standardized across projects and clients, and results are often embedded in a scalable platform. Commercially, the cost follows a rate card determined based upon the features and options included, such as the categories of analyses and the types of metrics.

By contrast, in a *service model* delivery, results are more likely customized to the request of the ultimate client, yielding bespoke solutions that closely meet the needs of a particular project. The service model also emphasizes consultative presentations of the insights found and consequent business recommendations. The cost is more likely to be based on labor time and materials.

- *Format*: This pertains to how the analytics results are actually delivered. In the product-based model, one popular option is a hosted, cloud-based software as a service dashboard, updated periodically according to a standardized schedule. Alternatively, a product can be delivered in a simpler format, such as a standardized "flat file" of a specific format that can be automatically transmitted or uploaded, or a standardized spreadsheet. The service model lends itself to interactive group meetings and workshops with discussion, supported by formal presentation slides.
- *Frequency*: Naturally, this specifies how often the results are delivered. In a product model, this usually follows a fixed, period schedule, such as monthly, weekly, daily, or even a live feed with refreshes as they occur by the minute (think stock tickers or sports scores). The delivery initiates once specifications have been gathered and the platform has been set up and run with initial data. Once setup, in principle results can be delivered indefinitely. In a service model, the delivery frequency and timing are dictated by the client's business milestones, such as brand planning, or major sales meetings. Also in a service model, the project duration is usually shorter, to reach particular conclusions. Once that project ends, a decision is made to end the engagement, standardize some of the custom work into a standardized product-type solution, or create a new custom project with associated but different objectives.
- *Customization*: This dimension relates to whether your actual analytics methodology and format of results are standardized, or are they specific to that client and project assignment. Consider an analysis like promotional campaign measurement, which we covered in a prior chapter. A completely standardized result would have fixed definitions for audience quality calculations, conversion metrics, and the layout of charts. A customized solution would make all of this and more at the specification of the project's client, who may feel that their own methods are critical for business

decisions and worth extra cost to develop. Such customization would be well beyond the typical variation allowed in analytic parameters, and dashboard menus and filters that show results at various levels of granularity.

11.2 Best Practices for Delivery Formats

To provide some context and dimension to this discussion, let's provide specific examples and guidelines to two primary delivery formats: a summary analytics dashboard and an analytics results presentation. These recommendations are based upon best practices I have observed across hundreds of projects and scenarios across industries.

11.2.1 Analytics Tracking Dashboard

The purpose of a standardized analytics longitudinal tracking dashboard, like that for a promotional campaign, is several fold:

- Provide an overview of performance at a glance
- Answer questions about the metrics stakeholders care about most
- Show trends over time
- Allow basic interactivity for those that want to explore further

In Figure 11.1 is a schematic that aims to achieve those goals with visual clarity. Let's navigate from top to bottom and describe each section with explanation of what they contribute.

The very top of the dashboard describes the business context and the purpose of the information, so there is no ambiguity. Below that are a few cumulative results on *key performance indicators (KPIs)*, which were likely agreed upon at project initiation when gathering requirements. While cumulative results are shown here, the latest time period's values are an alternative. The specific KPIs depicted in the figure are total campaign reach, percentage rate of audience quality, and a financial "lift" metric. These three were chosen as to all be meaningful, and also fairly independent of each other to capture different aspects of the campaign performance. Note that each of these is supplemented with a trend indicator, increase or decrease since the last reporting time period. This adds the additional context of how the campaign is performing recently.

The middle section summarizes specific variations within dimensions of primary interest to the audience as to what might be driving overall performance. There are summary distributions by customer segment, or audience segment, along one of the KPIs. There is also a geographic heat map showing which regions are most responsive. Again, specifics may vary based on your project; the geographies might be sales districts within a particular country.

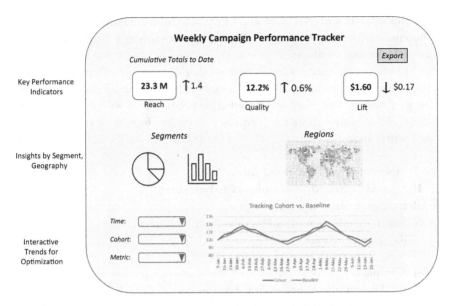

FIGURE 11.1   Typical Summary Campaign Tracking Dashboard

Finally in the lower section is an opportunity for users to see trends over time and to generate results at a more granular level. Navigation menus at left enable selection of a time range, a keymetric, and a cohort (such as media source, segment, attribute, or geography). The menus would be fed from summarized results tables and enable rapid, interactive drill-downs for quick comparisons. Results are shown vs. a *baseline* that could represent the prior year, or the overall campaign average.

Note while this may be considered a prototypical "summary page," there is room for variation based on one's style and the priorities of your project. Additionally, other pages can be added to the dashboard that go into more depth on specific business topics.

11.2.2 Analytics Results Presentation

Whatever your delivery business model, most likely you will be presenting results to the sponsors or the beneficiaries of your big data initiative. In this section, we will recommend a sequence and format for this talk, presuming you have 30 to 45 minutes to present.

One bias that many analytical experts or product managers make in business is crafting a presentation around their wares: focusing first on the analytical methodology or the product features. A related choice is starting with a demonstration of a dashboard early on. Admittedly, I have periodically succumbed to this urge. The problem may stem from academic training where showing methodology precedes results. The issue also may arise from lack of empathy for one's audience.

However, one must realize in business that the purpose of a presentation is to persuade one's audience, or to tell a story of how the brand and the business are performing. Therefore, the presentation needs to flow with the audience in mind. Below is a recommended sequence, in outline form with embellishment and justification.

I. Meeting purpose (how did we get here)
II. Agenda (optionally with timings and speakers)
III. Executive summary of findings
IV. Selected findings in detail (optionally an example)
V. Recommendations
VI. Next Steps (with owners and future timing)
VII. Appendix
    a.   Description of underlying data sources
    b.   Detailed analytics methodology
    c.   Analytical platform overview (for optional demonstration)
    d.   Additional detailed results

One should start any meeting with a concise background to its purpose, including business goals, and a short reminder of prior meetings and endorsements. No more than a slide should be spent on this, but then all in attendance will feel briefed, and confident the work has been authorized and endorsed before. Then an agenda on the next slide will further demonstrate professionalism and get the audience prepared to listen and focus the rest of the way.

Following this setup, some audience members may be eager, even impatient, to learn of the results. That is where the *executive summary* comes in to highlight the most significant data-driven results and the implications for future optimization and planning. Some participants may perk up and ask clarifying or challenging questions during the executive summary, but that should not trouble the presenters. Rather, view these questions as a sign of audience commitment to the project, and as an opportunity to show further detailed insights you worked so diligently to extract. We will come back to the executive summary shortly.

The next portion of slides is of variable length and presents the next level of detail on specific sections you feel will be compelling or actionable. Show cohort differences where optimization choices can be made, rather than those that are most statistically significant. Still avoid methodology details and algorithms; save those for later.

Afterwards, move on to recommendations: what promotional levers can be optimized, which channel should receive further investment, what other stakeholders should be notified, and should the pilot project be scaled up. These suggestions should yield active discussion or debate, and perhaps requests for additional backup results. A vested and perhaps skeptical audience will want to challenge your claims until they are convinced. Such a debate should naturally flow into the meeting "home stretch:" a list of next steps. This can include additional meetings with other stakeholders, follow-up analyses, or potentially planning operations for scale-up. Ideally, if time permits, this can be specified with owners, and timing to complete.

The Appendix is for additional slides that contain project details that could become relevant in answering a question or defending a summary point. Here is where you summarize background data sources, analytics methodology, as well as a demonstration of any relevant analytics platform. Also, keep here additional quantitative results not specified earlier, but which could be asked about. As a team, you should be prepared to show Appendix content when the conversation dictates.

With that overall structure defined, let's provide more detail on the notion of an Executive Summary. Over the years, I have come to prefer a structured, concise format, which summarized in Table 11.1.

The executive summary is a chance to state your data-driven conclusions in an organized fashion. List the core themes of the project or the analysis, followed by one or more conclusions that your analytics results suggest, with the key findings spelled out, and implications for next steps. In the table, for example, the theme of qualified reach shows a conclusion of a media source $m1$ with high-qualified reach at an efficient cost. Specific quantitative findings can be included as evidence. The implication is to shift media spending from underperformers to this superior media source. Other themes can proceed similarly. In a 30-minute meeting, there should be no more than four to five of these themes.

Some analysts may find it uncomfortable to go beyond generating output reports and recommend next business decisions. However, it is expected of

TABLE 11.1 Structure of an Executive Summary Table

Theme	Conclusions	Key Findings	Implications
Qualified reach	Media type $m1$ reaches qualified consumers at high volumes and efficient cost	A1 A2	Shift spending to $m1$ from underperforming media
Driving conversion	Creative c1 and offer $o1$ are optimal for generating new customers	B1 B2	Test $c1$ and $o1$ as alternative messages on more widespread media placements
Etc.			

analytics experts to at minimum propose these implications, to encourage the project sponsors to act upon the results.

One other point on high-stakes analytics meetings with clients or project sponsors: rehearsal is essential. This makes your language crisper and the presentation time shorter, allowing time for group discussion and decisions. Rehearsals give you the confidence to present without looking at the text and graphs on your slides, but rather engage the audience to judge their reactions.

11.3 Alternative Delivery Extremes

Now that we have spelled out the dimensions of big data analytics delivery, and exemplified core components, how can you decide the right mix for your analytics department, or consulting firm? Below we describe two extremes and the resulting implications.

11.3.1 Opposite Delivery Alternatives and Resulting Perspectives

Consider two alternatives at almost opposite ends of the spectrum, both having their merits, and both of which I have experienced as a provider and a consumer.

1. The **White Glove** approach is to deliver high-value customized presentations for each project that aim to deliver exactly the right insights for your audience.
2. The **Standardized Product** approach delivers results frequently and in standardized formats, usually employing a visual, cloud-based interactive dashboard.

In the white glove service, the primary emphasis is on value, quality, and impact. Less important is the time taken to create these results: a project may take weeks or months, and require multiple internal reviews and iterations before completion. A premium is placed on the *executive summary* that explicitly calls out the most insightful results and recommends the next course of action.

Consider the white glove service from two perspectives:

- From the point of view of the client receiving the analytics services, the white glover service is usually preferred, since the client can frame the project as bespoke, request customized metrics, and receives insights tailored to their particular business case. The primary trade-off for a client is the longer time to project results, and the likely higher project cost.

- From the vantage point of the analytics service provider, delivering as a white glove service requires more experienced staff that can anticipate different business questions and has skills in storytelling, linking the quantitative results to recommended decisions and actions. Indeed, producing the end presentations will require significant manual effort, interpreting the data, laying out results, and crafting recommendations. Automation and off-shore staffing will be at most a small part of the solution.

In the standardized product service, the emphasis is on throughput, efficiency, and reliability. Timing is crucial, and must be short-term and reliable. Automated data processing and quality control are essential. Results can be delivered weekly, daily, or more frequently. As such, there is minimal time for explicit review of results, or manually generated insights.

Now consider the standardized product service from the same two perspectives:

- From the point of view of the client, the standardized product model is favorable in yielding reliable results on a fixed schedule, and the cost being relatively less expensive per delivery. Typically, the results consist of numerical tables and charts, from which data can be extracted and used for other "in house" financial calculations. However, this places a burden on having client-side staff to interpret findings for making decisions.
- From the vantage point of the analytics service provider, the standardized product delivery model creates an opportunity for mass production and scalability. With proper design and automation, the same basic algorithms and visualizations can be applied to multiple clients, brands, and scenarios, at greater speed and higher project margins. The staffing mix can be shifted toward product managers, software developers, and off-shore contributors who need not be business domain experts. Also note there are two factors that can create organizational stress in delivery: the time pressure to meet the relentless delivery schedule, and the need for a strong quality control program that checks for accurate, consistent results to avoid error and re-work.

11.3.2 Successful Delivery in Practice: Migration from Extreme to a Blend

In my experience across different companies and analytics delivery leadership roles, I've learned that an optimal analytics delivery engagement is a blend of the white-glove and the productized approach. These are a few reasons why even a planned automation becomes slightly hybrid:

- At the start of an engagement, some requirements gathering is always necessary to judge how customized a solution can be, and what parameters need to be set.
- When results are delivered in an automated platform, the first few deliveries are optimal when a delivery specialist (or an account manager) can meet with clients to provide training on how to use the platform, describe the meaning of the results, and suggest interpretations.
- Then when the client is accustomed to the automated delivery system, the custom delivery and training needs decrease, and at most a standard "operational support" contract is required.

From the other direction, if starting with a custom analytics engagement with a presentation delivery, there should be a longer-term move toward standardization. Here is why:

- The most valuable results will spark business decisions like changes in sales or marketing strategy, communications, or promotional tactics.
- A natural consequence is wanting to follow up the initial analysis with ongoing tracking studies that re-evaluate the most salient metrics from the customized delivery. The goal is to see if the marketing actions taken have changed core metrics on a quarterly, semi-annual, or annual basis.
- Such repeated follow-ups can be standardized in simpler presentations and dashboards since the questions are established and the metrics consistent.

11.4 Business Use Cases with Blended Delivery Approaches

To further demonstrate to these analytics delivery principles, here are three brief business examples that describe how delivery adopts the hybrid approach.

11.4.1 Ongoing Media Campaign Reporting

Say you run a media agency placing display and video advertising via a series of targeting mechanisms: demographic and lifestyle websites, endemic content-specific information sites, behavioral re-targeting, and purchase-based propensity models. The goal for the campaign is to maximize the efficiency by which you can reach a qualified audience, defined by people likely to purchase.

Once a media campaign is initiated, ongoing performance tracking requires sizable data collection of impressions served and matching to separate repositories that can assess the quality of those receiving ads. This might be panel based, modelled out, or an actual one to one match to transactional behaviors.

TABLE 11.2 Typical Media Performance Tracking Output

Targeting Method	Media Cost	Cumulative Impressions	Digital Audience Reached	Percent of Audience that is Qualified	Qualified Audience Count	Cost Per Qualified Audience
Demographic	$50,000	2,272,727	916,313	12%		
Lifestyle	$75,000	3,000,000	1,279,963	10%		
Endemic media	$135,000	3,857,143	1,407,459	22%		
Behavioral Retargeting	45,000	4,090,909	1,641,571	30%		
Propensity models	75,000	6,250,000	2,683,852	20%		

Regardless, the outcomes produced on a weekly, or monthly basis can be summarized concisely as in Table 11.2.

We leave as an exercise to the reader the completion of this table. This table can also be represented graphically with bar charts or two-dimensional bubble charts in online dashboards.

While this table can be produced at scale in the long term, it will still require additional advice on how to optimize media spend given the findings. For this reason, for the first several time periods the tables and charts in the dashboards should be supplemented by a meeting and a consultative presentation that accomplishes the following goals:

- Outlines the campaign objectives
- Describes the targeting methodologies
- Explains why the media costs differ per targeting method
- Justifies the metrics of evaluation, including how is a quality audience determined
- Provide advice on media budget allocation changes

However, after several weeks once all users are accustomed to these metrics, these meetings may no longer be necessary, and the regular weekly online dashboard reports can be sufficient.

11.4.2 Field Force Effectiveness Tracking

There are many similarities between performance tracking of field force initiatives and the prior example of media campaign tracking. In both cases, the objective is to make optimal use of resources, in this case the field representatives' time and travel, to yield an optimal result of incremental sales.

In field forces, results can also be updated periodically with a regular cadence: weekly, monthly, or quarterly, depending on company culture and the decision-making cycle. There are (at least) three ways one can adapt Table 11.2 for such a purpose:

- Evaluate activity and performance of different customer segments per the calls made, and the resulting sales activity.
- Evaluate alternate messages or channels by the field representatives, to gauge impact on outcomes.
- Compare different field geographies (regions, districts, or territories) on calls per time period, overall and for specific customer segments.

As with the prior media example, production of the tracking tables and charts is not sufficient in the early stages. Collaborative discussions must take place among sales management, operations, and analytics consultants as to how to interpret the data and what conclusions and resource allocation decisions should be considered.

11.4.3 Competitive intelligence Tracking

When you are accountable for a brand's strategy in a dynamic and competitive category, it is critical to keep apprised of the in-market activity of companies selling competing products. I have led competitive intelligence functions for both manufacturers and product development companies and found the analysis and delivery needs as distributed and multifaceted.

The insights and interpretations within competitive intelligence can be somewhat subjective. For that reason, standardization is critical, including:

- Articles and press releases organized by topic
- Presentations by competitors at industry conferences
- Competitive product reviews
- Promotional creative, messaging, and media channel information

These should be presented as a mix of quantitative reporting tracking format, combined with examples and images available for supplemental interpretation. Samples can be indexed in a structured knowledge-sharing platform. In terms of the presentation, a standardized monthly report and discussion with strategic stakeholders can be quite effective. Since the content can be complex and multi-faceted, it is a good idea to send materials in advance.

11.5 Dynamic Factors to Delivery

One reality of big data analytics delivery is that there will be changes, some planned and others driven by your clients or internal stakeholders. Let's discuss two main sources of change and how you can anticipate and plan to adapt accordingly.

11.5.1 Deploying Analytics Innovation

Over time, it is natural to expect that your methodology for segmentation, predictive modeling, insights generation, and visualization may improve over time. Indeed, this is necessary for your group and your solutions to stay competitive and relevant. However, how do you introduce these updates to long-standing clients and existing operational processes?

One critical guideline is testing beforehand, to simulate the impact of a methodology update:

- Simulation to check if distinct results are produced with the new methods on prior inputs, and what the ramifications are. For example, would classifications change? Would there be fewer false positives?
- User acceptance testing to see if the updates in areas like visualizations will be accepted into practice.

Another guideline is providing transparency and time before implementing methodology updates. Notify your clients of any updated changes, and be ready to answer questions.

11.5.2 Handling Change Requests

One double-edged consequence of your analytics function delivering insightful findings is that these results may trigger additional questions, or re-framing of the original problem formulation. That yields requests for changes. The analytics translator, and the big data group leader, must determine whether these requests are material, specifically:

- Can the changes be handled readily with mere parameter changes in existing methods?
- Are alternative methodologies or data sources required?

The answer to these questions will dictate feasibility, timing, and cost of these changes.

11.6 Conclusions

In this chapter, we have considered important dimensions in delivering analytics results for genuine business impact, while maintaining a measure of efficiency. We highlighted that depending on how productized or customized your delivery methods are, there are implications for your staffing, your pricing structure, and the degree of customized satisfaction. Ultimately a hybrid model is usually most beneficial, with a leaning toward personalized attention in early project stages. The balance may depend on your industry, customers, and personnel, but should be explicitly planned for as you grow your big data analytics capability.

11.7 Exercises

1. Say you have a small analytics team serving multiple customers and projects in the same type of marketing analytics. You are successful but the team is stretched for time, and you've just learned that additional hiring budget is unlikely to come for another year.
   a) Which delivery method from this chapter would you favor: service oriented or product oriented? Why?
   b) What are some specific steps you would take to adjust for this additional demand.
2. Outline a short 20-minute business presentation per the guidelines in this chapter to deliver the results of an active analytics project you are working on. Alternatively, adapt a presentation given over the past year.
   a) Which core findings would you put in the Executive Summary?
   b) Which details would you move to the Appendix?
3. Complete the figures in Table 11.2 for the media tracking analysis, and then
   a) Calculate the two rightmost columns
   b) Design one or more charts that visualize key insights
   c) Suggest potential shifts in media dollars for the next time period.

12
SCALABILITY AND LONG-TERM SUCCESS

This chapter will step through solving core challenges in moving from early stage pilot success of big data analytics to designing and delivering scalable solutions. That means developing a repeatable system capable of handling tens or hundreds of times higher data volumes and delivering impact throughout an entire enterprise.

12.1 Moving Beyond Pilot Success

Once you've achieved success with a pilot leveraging big data and analytics, the typical response from your company stakeholders, or clients, will be: "How can we scale this up to the entire organization?" In this section, we will provide examples that demonstrate the steps required to meet this challenge.

12.1.1 The Need to Generalize and Expand

Let's revisit two of the running examples from this book to consider what is needed to expand from a pilot to a general scaled up rollout.

1. *Field force intelligence*: The pilot program might be an integrated sales report that integrates traditional and innovative data sources, and identifies sales leads for a core product leveraging forecasting. The pilot distribution was to one sales district, and key metrics were compared to another matched control sales district of similar geography and market dynamics. The results after 3 months in the pilot group showed a shift in sales representative call patterns toward targets, and a lift in sales vs. the control.

DOI: 10.4324/9780429300363-15

- After the pilot, the question is, how can this innovative sales targeting report be scaled-up to a monthly delivery for national field force, covering all major divisions and the products they sell?

2. *Digital media tracking and optimization*: The pilot program was developing a media tracking dashboard that evaluated digital advertising for one of your online consumer brands, showing for each of your digital channels (search, social, display, email) critical metrics like qualified reach, cost efficiency, and contributions to new product conversions. The pilot program lasted 3 months during which dashboard adoption was high, and your recommended optimizations were enacted and led to significantly improved media efficiencies and conversion rates.

- After the pilot, your challenge, how I can replicate this multi-channel digital dashboard across all brands in my company's marketing portfolio?

It is also safe to assume that for either pilot project there may be requests for updates, including changes and customizations of metrics, as well as slight alterations in the visualizations of the reports and dashboards.

12.1.2 Correcting for Pilot Overfitting

The factors that contribute to a successful pilot are sometimes at odds with requirements for scalability. In a pilot, the goal is to rapidly leverage the novel, integrated data sources or intelligent analytics and prove the case in a real-world scenario. What you seek is rapid feedback as to relevance and actionability. That feedback is necessary to judge commercial viability and to add to your queue of future enhancements. However, the rapid deployment usually comes via shortcuts, including the following:

- Specific category definitions and metrics calculations for the particular pilot case
- Programming scripts with "hard coded" variables particular to those pilot cases
- Customized dashboard charts and visualizations showing that brand or geography
- Manual data processing to populate dashboards and reports
- Delivery of results via email, or printed for in-person discussion

For case (1) above, these shortcuts may translate to the sales intelligence report emphasizing particular customers, or demographics primarily found in those pilot sales districts. For case (2), the digital optimization report may emphasize findings for channels specific to that campaign, or to that brand's stage in the product life cycle.

Shortcuts like these present a weakness of *overfitting* for particular pilot situations, and are not tenable as you scale up from say, two pilot cases to a broader rollout covering hundreds of productized deliveries on a continual basis. A different mindset, design, and execution are required for that magnitude of scalability.

12.1.3 Technical Project Phases

In a landmark discourse on what drives technical product success (Pinto and Slevin 1987) note that there are four phases for a technical project, with approximate levels of effort (measured by time or monetary investment) indicated as follows:

1. Conceptualization (10%)
2. Planning (30%)
3. Execution (45%)
4. Termination (15%)

The authors note that for most technical projects the level of effort, time, and monetary investment is skewed most heavily toward execution, and second within planning. Indeed, this seems appropriate for a one-time project, such as a pilot within big-data analytics.

However, consider the objective of a new steady-state, scalable solution built upon a foundation of efficient, high throughput operations. Execution time must be reduced in the long run to become swift and standardized, so that resources do not grow linearly with deliverables. The conceptualization might take on a larger share and become more like customer configuration. So-called termination actually morphs into ongoing customer support and enhancements.

When framed this way, it is clear that progressing from a pilot project to a scalable high-throughput product requires re-design and re-engineering of the prototype solution for mass-production. This re-tooling is the focus of the next section of this chapter.

12.2 Re-Designing for Modularity

When you are planning a scalable solution, it helps to anticipate and consider the broad range of clients and use cases that your solution must support. For sales and marketing analytics solutions, this includes planning for areas like:

- What is the range of product categories to support?
- What customer segments will I be analyzing?
- What promotional channels will I be measuring?

- What profiles of users will access my results, and what types of information will they consume?

Once you have set boundaries around what is the universe of your analytics deliverables, that can help guide the redesign.

12.2.1 Parameterization and Configuration

Carefully consider the delivery scenarios that stem from answering the above questions. In your solution, these are questions you must answer to shape each delivery. In short, these are configuration parameters that must be set whenever you onboard a new client or new project.

The parameters can be filled in as part of an onboarding process that gathers new project information from a combination of kickoff workshops, detailed forms, background research, and automated data ingestion.

One example to make this concrete: combing back to scenario (1) of field force intelligence tracking solutions, the onboarding process would include obtaining information regarding:

- Sales force alignment details, including geographic hierarchies for country, region, district, etc.
- Customer and Prospect segmentation codes
- Product names and codes
- Sales outcome metrics

Some of these inputs may be provided by analytics clients upon request, while others can be automatically extracted from complementary systems. In scenario (1), a salesforce automation or CRM system can be automatically queried to provide certain critical fields.

12.2.2 System Architecture Supporting Scalability

Your scalable solution should translate the parameters that are gathered at onboarding into explicit database dimensions and coding variables. See the partial schematic illustrated in Figure 12.1, where a dimension table is created for each campaign to be analyzed, and that table can be joined to additional dimension tables for product, category, channel, and geography. Any given project has a single row in the Campaign table with a *Campaign ID,* which serves as a join field to the other tables that supply additional details.

In terms of programming the analyses and metrics of the solution, see the right of the figure for "pseudo code" that spells out the calculation of market share for a time period, a channel, and a field geography. The code uses the campaign as an explicit parameter, and then evaluates the metric using the

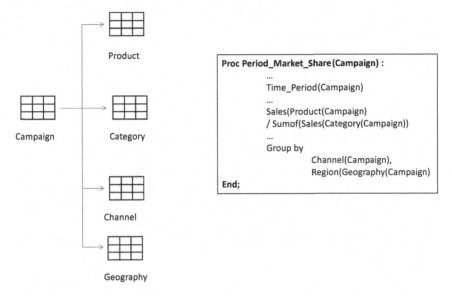

FIGURE 12.1 Partial Architecture for a Scalable Analytics Solution

specific values dictated from the joins of the dimension tables. In the exercises, we invite the reader to fill in additional details.

Note the differences between this design and the choices that might have been made for a one-time solution. In the latter case, the details of the different parameters would likely have been implemented within the analytics script, which is completely project specific. Now, they are in dimension tables that can be updated per hundreds of standardized projects, and the code can remain unchanged.

12.2.3 Process Automation

To reach a scalable solution that can deliver multiple projects at high throughput, an analytics leader must drive a relentless goal of automating manual processes. A sample of these are:

- Automatically connecting to input data sources via application programming interfaces (APIs)
- Cleansing, transformation, and aggregation of inputs to support analytics models
- Linking of analytics outputs into data visualizations and other client-ready file exports
- Quality control of analytics outputs, to which we will devote a section within this chapter

Such automation has the additional benefit of reducing labor costs and the potential for human error.

12.3 Quality Control Systems

When delivering a pilot project for a particular brand, sales district, or client, you can expend extra care in personally double-checking the work to look for accuracy and consistency. Not so when you are delivering to dozens of hundreds of clients. That is why *quality control* discipline is critical.

Usually when you think of quality control, manufacturing environments come to mind, with supervisors on factory floors measuring samples to ensure that defects are minimized, even nearly eliminated. Indeed, during my days at General Electric Research and Development under the leadership of CEO Jack Welch, virtually the entire company was trained in the Six Sigma methodology. This section will overview my experience on how quality control can be applied to analytics services.

Six Sigma is a valuable discipline largely because of the quantitative rigor. More details on the methodology and applications can be found within the Six Sigma Daily blog, or a number of textbooks or training courses, such as Gitlow (2015). More detailed training requires time investment and is rewarded by credentialing (via "belts:" green, black, etc.). One core analytic framework is *DMAIC*, for understanding variable processes and bringing them under control:

- *Define*: model the business process as a series of stages and determine the critical to quality (CTQ) metrics from the customer and business perspective. CTQs can include cost, time efficiency, or defect levels.
  - Note that a "six sigma" defect level is 3.4 parts per million opportunities! Defining the defect parameters is critical here. Is an opportunity every figure on every report? Every customer page view of your dashboard? Even if not achieving full six sigma levels, the goal is to reduce defects substantially.
- *Measure*: specify and accumulate data on all inputs and intermediate process variables that could affect the critical to quality outputs. Set up ongoing data collection process at regular time intervals.
- *Analyze*: using the collected process data, determine what the root causes are of the uncontrolled defective cases, and the reasons for poor levels of CTQ outcomes.
- *Improve*: implement changes that will address the root cause of problems, reduce errors, and improve CTQ results.
- *Control*: continuously monitor your business process with CTQs and key driver variables, to keep them within tolerable limits.

Control is maintained in part by implementing ongoing statistical process control charts where one monitors key variables over time within upper (UCL) and lower (LCL) numerical control limits. An example is depicted in Figure 12.2, for a weekly tracking metric that is supposed to be within the range of 5.2–5.8. Observations outside of these ranges would trigger alerts for further investigation.

Six Sigma and quality control are applicable to analytics services whether your analytics solution is consultative or productized, but gain in importance as your solution deployment scales. Here are several guidelines on bringing quality control formalisms into all phases of analytics services:

- *Analytics delivery dashboards*: CTQs include accuracy, completeness, and timely delivery of the dashboards. Missing or inaccurate data may be due ultimately to back-end calculation errors or data loading problems. User experience metrics should also be tracked, including page load times or login success rates.
- *Market research reports and presentations*: At a detailed level, you can consider the quality of your results based on reducing proofreading errors. More strategically, you can track the percentage of the "key insights" that you present which are found valuable by your clients; alternatively, reducing the insights that are disputed by clients.
- *Customer service response times*: How quickly are your data integrity specialists, or methodology experts responding to client questions? Internal sales team questions? Can you reduce the number of questions proactively through FAQ documents and improved training?
- *Chatbot or decision support recommendations*: Chatbots are a newer technology, based on natural language processing and machine learning. A good CTQ here is reducing the rate of rejected suggestions, or reducing mid-stream abandonment rates.
- *New business proposals*: For those in agencies, consultancies, or other analytics service providers, a critical portion of your time is spent replying

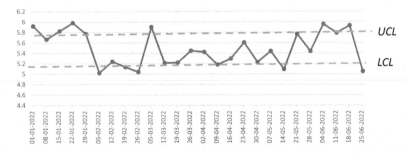

FIGURE 12.2 Process Control Chart Example, with Control Limits

to requests for proposals (RFPs) from potential clients. Responses include capabilities, case studies, and even complimentary work specific to the RFP criteria. The win rate, finalist rate, and person-hours of effort are all CTQs worth tracking and improving. These can be correlated with the components of the responses, to see if there are strong relationships that can lead to improvements in win rate and time efficiency.

- *Agile product development*: Product managers should embed quality CTQs into the specifications of upcoming version releases. Consider adding these to testing and evaluation criteria of the associated sprints.
- *One final word*: implementing six sigma in any business environment is definitely a team effort. This requires multiple parties to redesign systems or change their workflows to gather critical process data, and open themselves up to inspection. Collaboration and a common drive to improve business outcomes is critical for success.

12.4 A Closed Loop Learning Cycle

As your analytics organization deploys an increasing volume of analytics projects, it is critical to get increasingly more knowledgeable and sophisticated to gain improved insight and return each time. Figure 12.3 shows the supporting framework of a closed loop analytics cycle.

This methodology of *Plan, then Execute, then Measure and Optimize* is akin to closed-loop measurement for a series of promotional campaigns, where the primary optimization would be re-directing budget to the highest returning channels and media segments. At a higher level for an analytics, sales or marketing department, the goal is to optimize your decision-making methodology, and your choice of analytics projects, based on what has been learned from

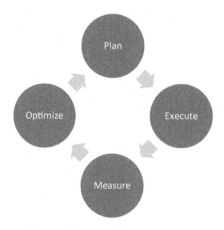

FIGURE 12.3 Closed Loop Analytics Cycle

prior projects. Knowledge management is a critical tool for driving that improvement, and we delve further in the next section.

12.5 Knowledge Management for Organizational Intelligence

For a company to attain mastery of big data analytics, it must continually learn from each project and delivery, both successes and failures. Formalizing this learning includes developing benchmarks of results, project meta-data for finding the right case studies, and communicating expertise as thought leadership. All of these will support the ultimate scalability objectives: each successive project should gain improved performance.

As an example, when you deploy media campaigns over time across a portfolio of products, then your performance improves, as measured by:

- Increased efficiency such as cost per qualified lead
- Widened conversion funnels, say the ratio from the initial media exposure to product conversion.

Additionally, analytics projects should become more time-efficient and higher quality. In predictive modeling, this can mean:

- Goodness of fit increases because of improved representation or modeling methods, or
- Analytics projects are completed more quickly due to a reduction in re-work from negative feedback.

To achieve this progress, the investment must be made to invest in organizational learning from your big data projects. In effect, each project, each predictive model, each media investment becomes an observation in itself. If you can centrally gather and represent dozens, hundreds, even thousands of such project-related observations with input parameters and performance metrics, then you can answer the following exciting questions to make your organization smarter:

- What prior cases have we analyzed similar to this one, and what were the outcomes in those cases?
- Can we statistically summarize benchmarks to predict and evaluate future performance, based on a similarity set across projects in the same promotional dimensions (media, product lines, audiences)?
- What are the attributes of a project that most drive a successful execution?
- Imagine the progress your company will feel operating in this fashion, continually learning, improving, and optimizing from prior experience. The rest of this section describes how to head down this path.

12.5.1 Representing Each Big Data Analytics Project

The first stage of learning from big data projects is to determine the representation of a project itself. An analytics group leader must consider what project attributes to capture for maximal learning and future optimization.

As a use case, consider target marketing offers within financial services, such as for consumer credit cards. Each offer is sent by direct mail or email to a set of consumer prospects. The actual substance of the offer includes a credit line (maximal spend amount), and the interest rate (percentage charged on unpaid balances). There may be other financial factors like balance transfer fees, but we will omit those for now.

A project record should include the business background. including:

- Project date range
- Product category
- Featured brand
- Project objective (if concisely expressible, such as new customer acquisition, cross-sell, re-activation, or loyalty)
- Size of consumer target population.

The record should also include the controllable "input" parameters that could in principle be changed in the future. For example, these can include:

- Creative imagery
- Messaging theme, and
- Offer details, including the interest rate and credit limit specifications

You should also include summary details of the analytical techniques applied within the project. In this example, how were the consumers selected for the credit card offer, was the selection based on

- Random selection
- Behavioral segmentation from prior transactions (especially valid for a re-contact or an up-sell campaign)
- Predictive models, such as decision trees, random forest, logistic regression, neural network.

Then, of course, the project record has to include the outcomes, such as

- Open rate of the messages, by channel
- Response rates, such as unique visitors to the website, unique callers to the toll-fee number, and unique response mailers
- Conversion rates to new accounts (or re-activated accounts) from the responders,

TABLE 12.1 Layout of a Project Database for Knowledge Management

Project Context	Input Parameters	Analytics	Outcomes

In summary, a project record has the layout of Table 12.1.

This basic layout can be employed across other business applications in various industries. Here are a few I've had experience with:

- In consumer auto insurance, a similar consumer targeting project framework applies as in credit cards. Some differences include the messaging, which might include cost savings, bundling of insurance, speed of claims response, or customer satisfaction, and the offer could include the premium cost and coverage levels.
- In consumer packaged goods, price sensitivity analysis is a frequent revenue growth analytics application that measures a response in sales volume per price change. The technique is usually regression modelling over a significant time period (which can be an analytics parameter). The outcome could be a recent sales lift for a brand that took a pricing action.
- In field-force driven sales, the knowledge management database could capture customized messaging of the field force (or the e-detailing), the method of segmenting the accounts, and the outcome is the aggregated incremental change in product prescribing.

12.5.2 Knowledge Management from the Project Database

With the project database established, there are a range of derivative analyses that can leverage this information. We list these below with examples.

- *Benchmarking*: Taking basic summary statistics of the project cases within a marketing category yields benchmark values and ranges for comparing future results. Summary statistics include the mean, median, range, and standard deviation. Let's revisit the CPG price elasticity example, and hypothetically consider the salty snacks category: say the average price elasticity measure across brands is -2.5 with a standard deviation of 0.4. This implies a price decrease of 10% could yield a short term sales increase of 21%–29% in the same time period, all else being equal with competition As another example, the Direct Marketing Association, has compiled and published industry response rates across delivery channels for years, gathering data by surveys to member companies.

- *Time trending of results*: A knowledge management database lets you discover shifts in analytics performance or market responsiveness over time. Examples of this are a decreasing click-through rate to paid search ads or email ads due to digital saturation.
- *Case based reasoning*: When there is a hypothetical new analytics project under consideration, then the knowledge management database can help estimate the possible results. By applying case-based reasoning, first you extract the cases from the database that are closely matched in multiple dimensions. Think of nearest neighbor matching. The small result set of matching cases can either be averaged for an estimated result, or a range can be taken for possible options.
- *Selecting project inputs*: If in your database you have attempted multiple cases for the same brand and objectives, then the knowledge management database can help you for future scenarios. Select those relevant cases, and determine how the outcomes varied with respect to project inputs. For example, which creative or messaging yielded the most positive outcome for your auto insurance brand? Which analytic modeling approach and threshold provided the greatest lift curve, and ultimately a superior response rate?
- *Key driver identification*: Extending the previous point one further, with sufficient project history, one can view the knowledge management database as a data set for predictive modeling. Returning to Table 12.1, you have a set of observations with varying inputs and one or more outcomes, like sales lift or conversion rate. One can apply a regression, decision tree, or other model to relate the project parameters to the ultimate outcome. These machine learning techniques can identify what factors are most driving successful promotions. Note as a caveat that there is a presumption that the different data points are all generated from the same distribution, meaning minimal market shifting within the time scale of your case library.

12.5.3 Commercial Opportunities

A large database of case studies can even have commercial benefit, especially to an analytics supplier. First, benchmarks over large case sets demonstrate expertise in analytics and in sales and marketing promotion. Nothing instils confidence to a prospect like saying, "we have executed (or measured) this hundreds of times before, and these are the benchmarks for your category." This confidence can be translated to an advantage in a competitive proposal response.

Second, benchmarks or predicted outcomes could actually be sold in lieu of analytics projects. Some prospective clients may have modest budgets and cannot afford a full-fledged big data analytics project to execute a targeted marketing campaign, or measure in-market promotions. The knowledge management database can be sold at a discount to these prospects, informing that you have a set of recent cases within their category under similar circumstances, with a range of outcomes or results.

12.6 Conclusions

In this chapter, we have covered a broad array of disciplines required for transforming a big data analytics capability from an ad-hoc, sequential project provider to a scalable function that can deliver concurrent projects across an industry. These disciplines include scalable design, automation, quality control, closed-loop learning, and knowledge management. As someone who has witnessed initiatives in each of these areas across companies, I would suggest that any one can be a career-enhancement path for leaders within your growing organization, providing significant visibility and impact.

12.7 Exercises

1. Fill in the additional details of the partial architecture of Figure 12.1 to support a scalable field force activity and impact tracking solution.
   a) What are the fields that should be included in each table illustrated?
   b) Add more detail to the pseudo-code that computes a product market share by sales geography. What table joins are required? Write your solution in SQL or Python if knowledgeable.
2. You lead a big data analytics marketing group in the financial services industry. This could be consumer credit cards or auto insurance, for example. Over the past 2 years you have run over 100 prospecting marketing offers to a random 200,000 prospects from the same consumer list service. The marketing offers have had variations of: financial terms, channel (direct mail, email, and social), month, and creative. You have collected data on delivery volumes, response rates, and conversion to new policies or cards, and basic demographic profiles of the responders. Based on the learnings from this chapter, how can you best leverage this for.
   a) Becoming more efficient with marketing moving forward?
   b) Forecasting future offer performance?
3. Say you have compiled a database of marketing promotion projects over the past 3 years, each promotional campaign lasting 1 month. You have noticed the trends of response rates decreasing over time from 2% in the earliest cases to more like 1% in more recent months.
   a) What impact would this have on benchmarks or forecasts that you provide for upcoming campaigns?
   b) How would you handle cases in your multi-year project database that occur during extraordinary, unusual time periods? Consider for example marketing campaigns during pandemic lockdowns, as occurred with COVID-19 during 2020 and 2021.
   c) Would these be included for benchmarks, or case-based predictions?

REFERENCES

Anandarajan, M., Hill, C., & Nolan, T. (2019). *Practical Text Analysis: Maximizing the Value of Text Data*. New York: Springer Press.

Benes, R. (2019, July 25). *US healthcare and pharma digital ad spending 2019*. Retrieved from eMarketer: https://www.emarketer.com/content/us-healthcare-and-pharma-ad-spending-2019

Bengfort, B., Bilbro, R., & Ojeda, T. (2018). *Applied Text Analysis with Python: Enabling Language-Aware Data Products with Machine Learning*. (N. Tache, Ed.) Sebastopol, CA: O'Reilly Media.

Blankfein, E., Engel, G., & Joseph, J. (2017). Modeling Marketing Drivers in the Network Space. *Advertising Research Foundation Annual Conference*. New York.

Brooks, F. P. (1995). *The Mythical Man-Month: Essays on Software Engineering*. Boston, MA: Addison Wesley Longman, Inc.

Burns, B., Beda, J., & Hightower, J. (2019). *Kubernetes: Up and Running: Dives into the Future of Infrastructure (Second Edition)*. Sebastopol, CA: O'Reilly.

Carpenter, G., & Lehmann, D. (1985). A Model of Marketing Mix, Brand Switching, and Competition. *Journal of Marketing Research*, 22, 318–329.

Cespedes, F. V. (2014). *Aligning Strategy and Sales: The Choices, Systems, and Behaviors That Drive Effective Selling*. Boston, MA: Harvard Business Review Press.

Davenport, T., & Harris, J. (2007). *Competing on Analytics: The New Science of Winning*. Brighton, MA: Harvard Business School Press.

Dean, A., & Voss, D. (1998). *Design and Analysis of Experiments (Springer Texts in Stastics)*. New York: Springer.

Dillon, W., & Goldstein, M. (1984). *Multivariate Analysis: Methods and Applications*. New York: John Wiley and Sons.

Duda, R. O., Hart, P. E., & Stork, D. G. (2001). *Pattern Classification*. Hoboken, NJ: John Wiley & Sons, Inc.

Evans, V., & Haimowitz, I. (2021, April 13). *Obtain assurance your campaign works—and will lead to brand growth*. Retrieved from PM360: https://www.pm360online.com/obtain-assurance-your-campaign-works-and-will-lead-to-brand-growth/

Fisher, R.A. (1936). The use of multiple measurements in taxonomic problems. *Annals of Eugenics*, 7(II), 179–188.

Freund, R., & Wilson, W. (1998). *Regression Analysis*. San Diego, CA: Academic Press.

Fulgoni, G. M., & Lipsman, A. (2017, September). Are You Using the Right Mobile Advertising Metrics? How Relevant Mobile Measures Change the Cross-Platform. *Journal of Advertising Research, 57*(3), 245–249.

Furtado, J., Haimowitz, I., & Wurst, M. (2003). LNAI 2926; Knowledge Discovery in Databases and Agent-Mediated Knowledge Management International Symposium AMKM. *AMKM 2003: Lecture Notes in Computer Science*, 339–250.

Geron, A. (2019). *Hands-On Machine Learning with Scikit-Learn, Keras and TensorFlow*. Sebastopol, CA: O'Reilly.

Gitlow, H. S. (2015). *A Guide to Six SIgma and Process Improvement for Practitioners and Students (Second Edition)*. Old Tapan, NJ: Pearson Eduction.

Hagiu, A., & Wright, J. (2020, January-February). When Data Creates Competitive Advantage... and When It Doesn't. *Harvard Business Review, 98*(1), 94–101.

Haimowitz, I. (2004). Criteria for Evaluating Data Mining Software. *American Pharmaceutical Review*, 7, 112–115.

Haimowitz, I. J. (2011). *HealthCare Relationship Marketing: Strategy, Design, and Measurement*. New York: Gower Publishing Company Limited.

Haimowitz, I. (2021). Media Measurement: How Much Are You Learning? *PM360*, October 2021.

Haimowitz, I., Gur-Ali, O., & Schwartz, H. (1997). Integrating and Mining Distributed Customer Databases. *Third International Conference on Knowledge Discovery and Data Mining*, 179–182.

Haimowitz, I., & Kemper, W. (2018). Applying Real-World Evidence Data for Measuring Pharmaceutical Digital Media Programs. *Journal of the Pharmaceutical Management Science Association*, 6.

Haimowitz, I., Le, P., & Kohane, I. (1995, December). Clinical Monitoring Using Regression-Based Trend Templates. *Artificial Intelligence in Medicine, 7*(6), 473–496.

Haimowitz, I., & Obata, C. (2009, May). The Science of Eavesdropping. *Medical Marketing and Media, 44*(5), 57–59.

Haimowitz, I., & Schwartz, H. (1997). Clustering and Prediction for Credit Line Management. *AAAI Workshop on Fraud Detection and Risk Management*, 29–33.

Han, J., & Kamber, M. (2006). *Data Mining: Concepts and Techniques (Second Edition)*. Morgan Kaufmann.

Hanssens, D. (2015). *Empirical Generalizations about Marketing Impact (Second Edition)*. Marketing Science Institute.

Harris, M., & Tayler, B. (2019, September-October). Don't Let Metrics Undermine Your Business: An Obsession with the Numbers Can Sink Your Strategy. *Harvard Business Review, 97*(5), 63–69.

Hartshorn, S. (2016). *Machine Learning with Random Forests and Decision Trees*. Kindle Unlimited.

HBR (2011). *Harvard Business Review on Greening Your Business Profitably*. Harvard Business Review Press.

Henke, N., Levine, J. and McInerney, P. (2018). You Don't Have to Be a Data Scientist to Fill This Must-Have Analytics Role, Harvard Business Review.

Howard-Grenville, J. (2021). ESH Impact Is Hard to Measure - But It's Not Impossible. *Harvard Business Review*, Jan 2021.

Iansiti, M., & Lakhani, K. R. (2020, January-February). Competing in the Age of AI: How Machine Intelligence Changed the Rules of Business. *Harvard Business Review, 98*(1), 61–67.

Klosowski, T. (2021, September 6). The State of Consumer Data Privacy Laws in the US (and Why It Matters). *The New York Times | Wirecutter.*

Lohr, S. (2021, July 17). *What ever happened to IBM's Watson?* Retrieved from *The New York Times:* https://www.nytimes.com/2021/07/16/technology/what-happened-ibm-watson.html#:~:text=At%20the%20end%20of%20last, Memorial%20Sloan%20 Kettering%20Cancer%20Center

Makridakis, S., Wheelwright, S., & Hyndman, R. (1998). *Forecasting: Methods and Applications (Third Edition).* New York: John Wiley and Sons.

McDonald, S. C. (2018, March). What Do We Really Know about Attitudes Toward Privacy and Advertisement Avoidance? *Journal of Advertising Research, 58*(1), 75–76.

Meharizghi, T., Cheong, L. L., & Calvo, M. R. (2021). Clinical Text Mining Using the Amazon Comprehend Medical New SNOMED CT API. *AWS Machine Learning Blog.*

Miller, M. (2021, September 15). *Delivering brand relevancy through connected data and analytics.* Retrieved from Pharmaceutical Executive: https://www.pharmexec.com/ view/delivering-brand-relevancy-through-connected-data-and-analytics

Moorman, C. (2019). *The CMO Survey: Highlights and Insights Report.* Deloitte, Duke, AMA.

Neufeld, E. (2017, March). Cross-Device and Cross-Channel Identity Measurement Issues and Guidelines: How Advertisers Can Maximize the Impact of an Identity-Based Brand Campaign. *Journal of Advertising Research, 57*(1), 109–117.

Oakland, J. (2008). *Statistical Process Control (Sixth Edition).* New York: Routledge.

Pinto, J. & Slevin, D. (1987). Critical factors in successful project implementation. *IEEE Transactionson Engineering Management, 34*(1), 22–27.

Provost, F., & Fawcett, T. (2013). *Data Science for Business: What You Need to Know About Data Mining and Data-Analytic Thinking.* Sebastopol, CA: O'Reilly Media.

Rahman, M., Rodriguez-Serrano, M., & Lambkin, M. (2017, December). Corporate Social Responsibility and Marketing Performance: The Moderating Role of Advertising Intensity. *Journal of Advertising Research, 57*(4), 368–378.

Schwartz, L., & Woloshin, S. (2019). Medical Marketing in the United States, 1997–2016. *JAMA, 321*(1), 80–96.

Snyder, J., & Garcia-Garcia, M. (2016, December). Advertising across Platforms: Conditions for Multimedia Campaigns: A Method for Determining Optimal Media Investment and Creative Strategies across Platforms. *Journal of Advertising Research, 56*(4), 352–367.

Sylvester, A. K., & Spaeth, J. (2019, June). Precise Targeting Foiled by Imprecise Data: Why Weak Data Accuracy and Coverage Threaten Advertising Effectiveness. *Journal of Advertising Research, 59*(2), 133–136.

Thomke, S. (2020, March-April). Building a Culture of Experimentation: It Takes More than Good Tools. It Takes a Complete Change of Attitude. *Harvard Business Review, 98*(2), 40–47.

Vigliarolo, B. (2021, October 1). *Consumer privacy study finds online privacy is of growing concern to increasingly more people.* Retrieved from TechRepublic: https:// www.techrepublic.com/article/consumer-privacy-study-finds-online-privacy-is-of-growing-concern-to-increasingly-more-people/

Wei, W. (2005). *Time Series Analysis: Univariate and Multivariate Methods (Second Edition)*. San Franscisco: Addison Wesley.

Weiner, M., Arnorsdottir, L., Lang, R., & Smith, B. (2010). Isolating the Effects of Media-Based Public Relations On Sales: Optimization Through Marketing Mix Modeling. *Institure for Public Relations*.

Zhao, K., Mahboobi, S., & Bagieri, S. (2018). Shapley Value Methods for Attribution Modeling in Online Advertising. *EconPapers*, 4.

INDEX

A/B testing 83
addressable media 71, 121
adstocking 81
agile development 33, 44, 148
Amazon 14, 59, 96–100
application programming interface (API) 31, 117, 145
ARIMA models 108–109
ARMA models 108
attribution 80–85, 90, 125

backpropagation 109–100
base sales 81
billability 43
binary classifiers 97, 102, 106, 114–118
bridge file 123
business intelligence 5
business process 5–9, 19, 103–106, 116–117, 128, 46

campaign design 11–12
campaign measurement 12, 75, 77–89, 125, 129
capabilities grid 44–47
case-based reasoning 152
change requests 139
churn 41, 102, 106, 114–118, 139
classification 3–4, 17, 32, 96–98, 101–102, 106, 110–118
client-side environment 39, 44, 47, 135
cluster analysis 3, 11, 32, 55–61, 92, 96
competition 41, 80, 151

competitive intelligence 34, 66, 92–95, 128–138
configuration parameters 143–144
constraints on big data projects 4–7, 57, 85
consulting firms 7, 42–43
consumer packaged goods 10, 37, 40, 51, 62, 71, 95, 108, 123–124, 151
cookies 123–127
cost efficiency 11, 19, 21, 25, 31, 63, 70–73, 88–90, 103, 142
credit analysis 4, 9, 15–17, 23, 25, 52–57, 60–62, 72, 85, 103, 106–107, 112–116, 126, 150–153
crisis monitoring 98
cross-validation 106
crosswalk file 123–125
customer journey 11, 76–77, 84, 88, 103, 124
customer segments 12, 38, 51–55, 63, 130, 138, 143
customized communications 62

dashboards 5, 6, 16, 18, 22–25, 32, 41, 128–137, 142, 146–147
data engineering 10, 58, 62, 81, 104–105, 128
data privacy 71, 85, 121
data science 3–6, 29, 38, 62, 104–105
denormalized tables 53–54, 58, 104–105
design of experiments 68, 83
designated market area (DMA) 80
development operations 30–31

direct marketing 75, 83, 151
display advertising 68–69, 74, 77, 79, 81, 121, 136, 142
distance metric 55–59, 112

early adopters 52
eligibility 85

factor analysis 11
feature extraction 32, 97
financial exposure 16, 61
forecasting 4, 11, 20, 25–26, 34–35, 105–108, 112, 141, 153
fractional factorial 83

Glassdoor 95

hash key 123, 126
holdout sample 56, 80–82, 97

IBM Watson 14, 98
identity resolution 122–125
insights generation 10, 32, 139

justifying investments 14, 18–21, 25, 27, 34, 40

Keras 117
key performance indicators 32, 75, 78, 103, 130–131
Kubernetes 117

life cycle, product 142
litmus test 60
logistic regression 9, 107, 112, 115, 150
logit 107
loss function 111

machine learning 8, 47, 72, 89, 97–101, 106, 117, 147, 152
machine learning operations (ML Ops) 106
market research 5, 25, 34, 60, 87, 98–100, 127, 147
marketing mix analysis 80–81, 107
marketplace intelligence 11, 94
matrix organization 40–41
measurement plan 75–77, 80–81, 84, 88–89
media optimization 128
methodology updates 139
milestones 6, 19–25, 46, 129

National Advertising Initiative (NAI) 124

natural language processing 4–5, 31, 100, 147
nearest neighbor 57, 152
net promotor score 17
neural networks 5, 97, 109–110, 150
next best action (engagement) 12, 62, 66

onboarding 144
oncology 118
overfitting 105–106, 142–143

pandemic 43, 66, 71, 75, 153
partition 53; *see also* segmentation
personas 18, 26, 61
pharmaceuticals 18, 40, 53, 62, 65–66, 71–78, 87, 96, 100, 124, 151
pilot projects 14, 20–26, 142–143, 146
pitch presentations 43
political environment 41–42
price elasticity (sensitivity) 151
principal component analysis 11, 59
product development 28, 30–38, 44–45, 93, 138, 148
product features 10, 22, 30–36, 52, 69, 97, 101, 126, 129, 132
product lifecycle 10, 41
product management 31, 34–37, 44
product portfolio 9, 10, 55, 142, 149
project plan 9, 12, 19
Python 32, 41, 59, 85, 97, 104, 110–111, 117, 153

qualified audience 69–78, 84–85, 88, 90, 133, 136–137, 142, 149
quality control 16, 33, 46, 135, 145–147, 153

regression 9, 97, 107, 109–112, 115, 150–152; *see also* logistic
reputation analysis 5, 19, 91–95, 98, 128
request for proposals (RFPs) 42, 148
response rates 87, 150–153
return on ad spend (ROAS) 86
return on investment (ROI) 81, 85–86
review sites 99
risk management 16–17, 41, 56–57, 61, 113, 116–117
ROC curve 115–116
RRID, reverse re-identification assessment 126

sales forces 6, 8, 25, 61, 65, 128, 144
salty snacks 10, 123–124, 151
satisfaction, customer 16, 35, 42, 45, 151

sensitivity analysis 81, 97, 106, 114–116
sentiment analysis 4, 31–32, 44, 92–93, 96–101
Shapley analysis 85
significance testing 32
simulation 38, 81, 116, 139
six sigma 16, 146–148
social media 4–5, 31, 54, 58, 61, 63, 81, 92–96, 99
software as a service 129
software, commercial 15–21, 32, 39, 83, 96–98, 117, 129, 135
specificity 97, 114–116
statistical process control 147
storyboards 18–21
surveys 4, 75, 77, 80, 99, 121, 127

targeting index 71
taxonomy 10, 37, 95–95

Tensorflow 117
text mining 91–101, 152
thresholds 41, 55–58, 78, 98, 103, 112–116, 126, 152
time accounting 43
time series 80, 107–109
true negative rate 97, 114
true positive rate 97, 114–115, 118
Twitter, or tweets 5, 92, 97

unstructured data 4, 14, 31–32, 91, 93, 100; *see also* text mining
user acceptance testing 139

validation 6, 56, 97, 105–113, 116–118
virtual assistants 99

waterfall chart 81

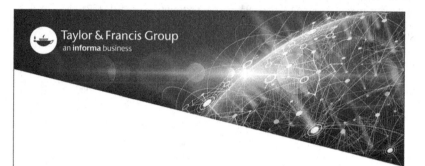

Printed in the United States
by Baker & Taylor Publisher Services